SCIENCE AND CREATION

Also by John Polkinghorne and published by SPCK:

One World (1986)
The Way the World Is (Triangle 1983)

SCIENCE AND CREATION

The Search for Understanding

John Polkinghorne

First published in Great Britain 1988
SPCK
Holy Trinity Church
Marylebone Road
London NW1 4DU

British Library Cataloguing in Publication Data

Polkinghorne, J.C.
  Science and creation: the search for understanding.
  1. Religion and science——1946-
  I. Title
  215   BL240.2

  ISBN 0-281-04344-2

Photoset, printed and bound in Great Britain by
WBC Print Ltd, Bristol

To the places of my Cambridge education

The Perse School
Trinity College
Westcott House

and to my teachers

CONTENTS

ACKNOWLEDGEMENTS

I am grateful to Principal Adam Neville and the University of Dundee for their invitation to give the Margaret Harris Lectures in Religion for 1987, which form the basis of this book. I am also grateful for hospitality given me while I was delivering the Lectures, particularly by Principal Michael Hamlin and by the University Chaplain, the Reverend Robert Gillies.

I thank my wife Ruth for help with correcting the proofs, and the editorial staff of SPCK for their assistance in preparing the manuscript for press.

Trinity Hall   John Polkinghorne
Cambridge.
December 1987.

. . . the very order, changes, and movements in the universe, the very beauty of form in all that is visible, proclaim, however silently, both that the world was created and also that its Creator could be none other than God whose greatness and beauty are both ineffable and invisible.

St Augustine, *The City of God*

INTRODUCTION

When I gave up being a professional physicist and became an Anglican priest, my life altered in many ways. Yet there were certain continuities amid the flux of change. What attracts young men and women to the study of the physical world, and holds them to it despite the weariness and frustration inherent in research, is the marvellous way in which that world is open to our understanding. I am somewhat of an adherent to the 'great man' theory of the history of science – that it is the insights of the men of genius which really propel the subject – but even those of us who only belong to the army of honest toilers share in the excitement as the pattern of nature is laid bare to human inquiry. In the 1950s the new particles discovered in cosmic rays were found to behave in ways which seemed more and more puzzling and perverse. Then Lee and Yang came along and suggested that maybe there is a preference in nature for the left hand over the right. Suddenly what threatened to be a perplexing chaos became a scene of beautiful order.[1] One can live on the intellectual satisfaction of having been a spectator of such an act of insight for quite a long time. It is the desire to understand the world that motivates all those who work in fundamental physics.

A similar desire is part of the inspiration for the religious quest. Of course the Nicene Creed and the Chalcedonian definition do not encapsulate God and Christ in the way that Clerk Maxwell could lay bare the essentials of electromagnetism when he wrote down his famous equations. The reality of God so far transcends our finite grasp that he will never be held by our intellects in such a way. Our encounter with him involves deeper levels within us than that of the rational mind alone and it demands a total response of obedience and worship. Nevertheless the search for understanding will be incomplete if it does not include within itself the religious quest, for otherwise it will leave fundamental questions of significance and purpose un-addressed and unanswered. Here is the point of continuity between the life of the physicist and the life of the priest, or better, between the scientific and theological questionings always contemporaneously present within one person.

I wrote my book *One World* to assert the unity of our search for understanding of the world in which we live. The book had two main thrusts to its argument. One was to discern the true natures of science and theology. Both are responses to the way things are and both proceed by conjoining logical analysis with intuitive acts of judgement. Ultimately each must defend its claim to be in touch with reality by an appeal to the coherent intelligibility it achieves through its insights. Science and theology have a fraternal relationship and they are complementary, rather than antithetic, disciplines. Yet each surveys the one world of experience from its own perspective and therefore there are possible points of contact, or even conflict, between them. The second thrust of my book was to consider the ways in which these two views of the world impinge upon each other and to suggest that their mutual interaction, though not free from puzzlement, is in fact fruitful and enhancing.

In the present volume I seek to carry the matter further. In *One World* the appeal was largely to very general theological ideas and to the coherent order of fundamental physics. Now my concern is to make contact with certain specific aspects of theological thinking and to explore those features of the physical world which arise from the behaviour of complex physical systems.

If it is true that theology is no mere speculative system but a response to what is, then surely it will always have been in need of cool appraisal of the world it seeks to understand. Natural theology – the search for God through the exercise of reason and the inspection of the world – is then not an optional extra, for indulgence by the scientifically inclined, but rather it is an indispensable part of theological inquiry. Chapter 1 seeks to confirm this view by a survey of the long history of natural theology (even among people as temperamentally averse to it as the ancient Hebrews) and of its revival today, despite the hesitations and timidity of many theologians.

The quest for sufficient reason and a comprehensive understanding of the world drives the physicist to seek unified theories which consolidate the forces of nature into a single grand scheme. The order and balance of the world so discerned often seems to speak to him of there being more to the universe than has met his scientific eye. Physics needs metaphysics for its intellectually satisfying completion. The evaluation of such a feeling calls for a careful discussion of significance and coincidence, which Chapter 2 seeks to supply. At its close it draws on the thought of Bernard Lonergan, for whom the search for understanding through and through is truly the search for God.

The world of fundamental physics has about it an air of timeless order. Its fitting 'god' might appear to be the God of Aristotle, in his unchanging perfection and his impersonal remoteness, or, alternatively, the rarefied pantheism of Spinoza's *deus sive natura*, which Einstein said was his deity. Yet out of that world of being which fundamental physics describes there arises the everyday world of becoming, the world of our direct experience, a world of disorder as well as order, whose fitting 'god' is closer to the God of Abraham, Isaac and Jacob. This level shift, from being to becoming, from dynamics to thermodynamics (to put it in physical terms), has become much better understood in recent years through the work of Ilya Prigogine and others. The modern conception of a world in which chance and necessity, symmetry and its spontaneous breakdown, interlace each other is presented in Chapter 3 (perhaps the most demanding part of the book).

This picture of the evolutionary process of the world poses certain questions for the Christian doctrine of creation. God is no longer seen as the cosmic Craftsman in complete control of his products and their consequences. Chapter 4 argues that the lawful necessity of the universe is to be understood as a reflection of God's faithfulness, whilst the role of chance in the world's process is a reflection of the precariousness inescapable in the gift of freedom by love. Such ideas prove strikingly consonant with the thoughts of W. H. Vanstone, arising from his consideration of the nature and costliness of creativity. They also relate to the endeavours of modern theologians, such as Ward and Moltmann, who seek to find a place within deity for both time and eternity, being and becoming.

If the twin disciplines of science and theology are to be united in fruitful harmony, together with those other insights such as art which lie between them in the spectrum of human inquiry, then one must attempt to find an account of reality capable of accommodating so wide a breadth of knowledge and experience. Chapter 5 rejects a materialist reductionism, or a retreat into idealism, or the unintegrated domains of Cartesian dualism. In their place it tentatively proposes a complementary metaphysic of mind/matter. The relations of these ideas to Moltmann's 'created heaven' and Popper's World 3 are noted and discussed.

If reason is, as John Murray said,[2] 'the capacity to behave in terms of the nature of the object' then both science and theology aspire to such a rationality. Chapter 6 discusses the resulting similarities, and also the necessary differences, between the two subjects. It seeks to illustrate how a scientifically-minded person approaches the task of theological inquiry (conceived as the search for understanding) by making the work of Christ the key to Christology and showing how the incarnation is the perfect fusion of symbol and event, of fact and interpretation.

1

Natural Theology

A scientist of even quite modest attainments will find from time to time that he receives unsolicited contributions from the general public proposing solutions to the riddle of the physical universe. His correspondents may need a little help with the mathematics or a testimonial to facilitate the publication of their ideas, but they are confident that they have made an important advance. I am sorry to have to say that such items of this character that have come my way have, without exception, proved valueless. Many have not been sufficiently articulate even to attain the status of being wrong. Nor does some kinship with science prove a help in the matter. Some of my most persistent and wrong-headed correspondents have been electrical engineers.

This thought crosses my mind as I, a theoretical physicist by profession, take up my pen to write on matters theological. To be sure I received some grounding in theology during my preparation for ordination and the subject remains among the principal interests which direct my reading, but it is also true that electrical engineers are taught a bit of physics and no doubt they read more about it after graduation. So how can I have the temerity to attempt the present task? I certainly cannot pretend to write as a professional theologian, but only as a scientist deeply interested in the understanding of religion.

I believe that the justification for the enterprise lies in the nature of theology. If it is to lay claim again to its medieval title of the Queen of the Sciences that will not be because it is in a position to prescribe the answers to the questions discussed by other disciplines. Rather it will be because it must avail itself of their answers in the conduct of its own inquiry, thereby setting them within the most profound context available. Theology's regal status lies in its commitment to seek the deepest possible level of understanding. In the course of that endeavour it needs to take into account all other forms of knowledge, while in no way attempting to assert an hegemony over them. A

1

theological view of the world is a total view of the world. Every form of human understanding must make its contribution to it. The offering of the physical sciences to that end must be made, at least partly, by those who work in them. Theology cannot just be left to the theologians, as is made clear by the recent spectacle of a distinguished theologian writing over three hundred pages on God in creation with only an occasional and cursory reference to scientific insight.[1] It is as idle to suppose that one can satisfactorily speak about the doctrine of creation without taking into account the actual nature of the world, as it would be to think that the significance of the world could be exhaustively conveyed in the scientific description of its physical processes. There must be a degree of consonance between the assertions of science and theology if the latter are to make sense and hence there is an urgent need for dialogue between the two disciplines. The arena for their interaction is natural theology.

Natural theology may be defined as the search for the knowledge of God by the exercise of reason and the inspection of the world. There are, of course, those who would deny the possibility of such knowledge. They are by no means all of an atheist or agnostic persuasion. People of religious belief have sometimes been so impressed by the transcendent otherness of God that they have asserted that he is only be to encountered in his gracious and specific acts of self-disclosure. He can condescend to us but we are powerless to reach out to him. The leading proponent of this point of view in our century has been Karl Barth, who wrote of the God of whom the Christian creeds speak that

> He cannot be known by the powers of human knowledge, but is apprehensible and apprehended solely because of His own freedom, decision and action. What man can know by his own power acccording to the measure of his natural powers, his understanding, his feeling, will be at most something like a supreme being, an absolute nature, the idea of an utterly free power, of a being towering over everything. This absolute and supreme being, the ultimate and most profound, this 'thing in itself', has nothing to do with God.[2]

That 'nothing' seems like something of an overstatement. We can acknowledge that natural theology, whose source of insight is by definition limited to the generalities of experience, will not tell us all about God that is humanly accessible. The individual encounter with him, both our own and that of the spiritual masters preserved in the tradition, will surely be of the highest importance. Yet the world is not just a neutral theatre in which these individual revelatory acts take place. Rather, it is itself, if theism is true, the creation of God and so potentially a vehicle also for his self-disclosure. God is to be found in the general as well as in the particular. Natural theology may only be able to help us to discern 'something like a supreme being, an absolute nature', and it is certainly powerless by itself to bring us to know the God and Father of our Lord Jesus Christ, but its insights are not for that reason to be despised. There is a great deal more to the structure of matter than chemistry can tell us, with its talk of ninety-two elements, but it would be foolish to refuse its assistance in an inquiry into what the physical world is made of. Similarly natural theology can provide valuable help in an inquiry about whether the process of the world is the carrier of significance and the expression of purpose. This role is of special relevance today when so many people find it difficult to see theism as a credible and coherent possibility. Natural theology may be for them a necessary starting-point. I agree with Hugh Montefiore when he writes about the relationship of the intellectual quest for God through natural theology to the personal commitment of faith, that

> while it is true that cold intellectual thinking can never bring anyone into a warm personal relationship with God, it is also true that, while a subjective commitment to God may be satisfying to the self, it lacks credibility to others unless it can be shown that there are good reasons for the actual existence of the God to whom commitment has been given.[3]

The contention that natural theology is important is supported by a consideration of the history of religious thought. I shall attempt a survey to show that it has had a continuing role within the Judaeo-Christian tradition.

At first sight no one could seem to be less concerned with such matters than ancient Israel. Belief that there is a God is absolutely axiomatic in the Old Testament (as it is in the New Testament). There is no attempt to reason the matter; no apologetic argument for God's existence. The priests proclaim that he is known in the worship he has ordained and the laws that he has promulgated. The prophets declare him to be found in his saving and judgemental acts in history. Yet even in Israel there were those who also sought him in the everyday circumstances of life, or who at least tried to make sense of humdrum experience in the light of their faith in Yahweh. The fruit of their labour is recorded for us in the wisdom literature of the Old Testament and Apocrypha. One of its characteristic forms of expression is the proverb, a sort of refinement of the folk adage. By this means the wise men sought to discern an order in the chaotic flux of events. Von Rad said that the wisdom teachers 'stood in the forward line of experiential knowledge'.[4] Their observation is often deadpan, without overt moralizing:

> A poor man is odious even to his friends;
> the rich have friends in plenty.[5]

They are men of patient observation rather than charismatic enlightenment, so that a certain calm level-headedness attracts their praise:

> Experience uses few words;
> discernment keeps a cool head.[6]

One feels that they would thoroughly approve of the motto of the Royal Society: *Nullius in verba* (freely translated – no mere talking). An anchorage in the way things are, acting as a restraint on speculative fancy, is of particular importance for theology. One is sometimes astonished at the confidence with which the Fathers or the medieval theologians will discuss such ineffable subjects as the nature of angels or the inner life of the Holy Trinity. The wise men encourage the asking of the question, instinctive to the scientist, How do you know? They look at the world with an openness to the hard facts of its reality and resist the temptation, endemic in religious thought, to confine oneself to the way one would like things to be or hopes that they will eventually come to be. Yet in pursuit of knowledge the wise men were willing to recognize their own limitations as part of what actually is the case. Von Rad says that they were 'aware that the area a man can grasp with his rational powers and tell out with his being is really small'.[7] Rational exploration did not decoy them into rational overconfidence:

> Face to face with the Lord
> wisdom, understanding, counsel go for nothing.[8]

4

Since the wisdom writers' special concern is with knowledge of God derived from general rather than particular experience, there is a universal character to their thought. The founding figure of the tradition was said to be Solomon and one can readily imagine such a warily appraising attitude arising in the cosmopolitan brilliance of his court. He is compared with the wise men from the East and from Egypt, admittedly to his advantage but in terms that suggest that like is being set beside like,[9] a comparison with other nations unthinkable for Israel in the spheres of priest or prophet. Part of the Book of Proverbs (22.17—24.22) is a transcription from the Egyptian writings of Amenemope. There is an accessible character to natural theology which helps it to cross cultic frontiers. Nevertheless, in the end it must seek its integration with the totality of the experience of God and of thought about him. The later wisdom writings are set in a more explicitly Yahwistic context than their predecessors.[10]

As part of the wise men's cool observation of the world there was regard for what we would call nature (a concept itself unknown to Hebrew). Thus at the end of the Book of Job, God's answer to the complaints of the innocent sufferer is a catalogue of the wonders of the physical world (Job 38, 39) and an injunction to consider the hippopotamus and the crocodile, albeit exalted to mythic proportions (Job 40, 41). They are reminders to Job that the Lord has other concerns beyond those with men: 'Behold, Behemoth, which I made as I made you.'[11] It is characteristic of natural theology that it delivers us from a narrow anthropocentricity. Moltmann is surely right to say that 'no theological doctrine of creation must be allowed to reduce the understanding of belief in creation to the existential self-understanding of the person. If God is not the Creator of the world, he cannot be my Creator either.'[12]

At a humbler level the enumeration sayings in Proverbs, such as

Three things are too wonderful for me;
four I do not understand:
the way of an eagle in the sky,
the way of a serpent on a rock,
the way of a ship on the high seas,
and the way of a man with a maiden[13]

show a concern with the physical world at the level of natural history,

5

the encyclopaedic collection of 'for instances'. The Hebrews were unable to proceed beyond this to develop a scientific point of view concerned with a pattern of cause and effect. They lacked the necessary concepts. In particular, despite experience of exile in Babylon (an ancient centre of some degree of sophistication in calculation and astronomy), they made no progress with mathematics. Nevertheless the post-exilic wisdom writers did take one remarkable step. They personified wisdom, speaking of her as the beginning of God's works, antedating the material world,[14] his agent in creation,[15] and his consort in its enjoyment.[16] This astonishing figure is a challenge to exegetes. Von Rad says that the wisdom imagery shows that God 'had at his service a quite different means, besides prophets and priests, whereby he could reach men, namely the voice of primeval order'.[17] Thus it was that natural theology found voice in the Old Testament.

Wisdom is one of the many concepts which constellate round the *Logos*, the Word, so powerfully proclaimed as being in the beginning with God and equivalent to God, in the prologue to St John's Gospel.[18] Ideas come together here which are both Greek and Hebrew in origin. The Stoic notion of the *logos* is concerned with the rational order of the world, whilst the Hebrew *dābār* (which means both word and deed) focuses on activity, that word of the Lord by which the heavens were made[19] and which came to the prophets as the message of God's purpose at work in history. The twin discernment of both pattern and process in the workings of the world, of being and becoming, lies at the heart of any attempt to construct a natural theology in true accord with the way things are. There has been a perpetual temptation in religious thought to concentrate on one pole or the other of this dialectic – the static perfection of the God of the philosophers, in all his remoteness; the living God of Abraham, Isaac and Jacob, in all his dangerous anthropomorphism. A true account will hold the two in balance. It is interesting that a similar complementarity of being and becoming is necessary in the scientific story of the world, as we shall see in Chapter 3.

Before John's prologue is completed he has moved from the generalities of form to the particularity of expression in making the quintessential Christian assertion that the Word became flesh and dwelt among us. The Epistle to the Colossians declares of the Christ so made known that 'he is before all things and in him all things hold together'.[20] Such consistency as we may find in the coherence of the world will never of itself lead us to the cosmic Christ of Colossians, but that cosmic Christ would not be believable if the universe were at root a chaos rather than a cosmos. There must be a congruence between the claims of revelation and the perceptions of a rational inquiry into the world. That necessity alone is sufficient to make natural theology an indispensable part of the theological endeavour.

The urban Christians who wrote the New Testament show less concern with the natural world than do the writers of the Old Testament whose style of life made them more in touch with nature. The New Testament writers are so seized by the thought of God's great act in Christ by which they have been encountered that the generalities of human experience play only a small part in their thought. Nevertheless it is Paul whose words provide the classic text to which natural theologians are wont to appeal in search of scriptural warrant for their activities. Writing to the Romans he held that no man can excuse himself on the grounds that he did not know that there is a God for 'Ever since the creation of the world his invisible nature, namely his power and deity, has been clearly perceived in the things that have been made'.[21] We might feel that the clarity of the case is somewhat exaggerated by Paul but his words certainly encourage the attempt to pursue a natural theology. God is the elusive hidden one, not overpowering us by his unveiled presence, but it would surely be disconcerting if there were no signs of him to be found in his creation.

The Greek Fathers of the Church made use of the idea of the *Logos*, particularly in the second century, as 'the answer to the problem of how God could be both a changeless self-contained being and at the same time the active Creator God'.[22] Their concern was with the dialectic of being and becoming, but concentrating on the question of how God is related to the world in a 'descending' movement, opposite to the 'ascending' flow of natural theology seeking to move from the world to God. As the Fathers continued their wrestling with the mysteries of the incarnation and the Holy Trinity, in an effort to do justice to the particular experiences of revelation, the *Logos* faded out as a useful category of thought. In the Western Church Augustine's great influence militated against the exercise of reason and the inspection of the world as routes to God. He wrote: 'Understanding is the reward of faith. Therefore do not seek to understand in order to believe but believe in order that you may understand.'[23] The one-sided emphasis is ironic in one who was the greatest intellect that the Latin Church produced and whose powers of introspection into the polarities of the human psyche provided him with the basis for the most penetrating discussion yet written concerning the doctrine of the Holy Trinity. The link between belief and understanding is a root concern of this essay. They cohere in mutual interaction which requires a balance in which neither is afforded an overriding primacy. The dialogue between them is analogous to that between theory and experiment in science. Without the insight of theory experiment would have no significance. The behaviours and registrations of laboratory apparatus are not of interest in themselves but only for what they are understood to signify. In a similar way an act of faith, a commitment to some belief, is necessary in the search for wider understanding. On the other hand no theory can survive which does not find some confirmation in experiment. A physical idea, however intrinsically beautiful, will only remain of interest if it proves capable of illuminating physical fact. In a similar way faith is not unmotivated. It must be congruent with the way things are and corrigible by them. There is an analogy between this dialectic of faith and understanding and the interrelationship of divine grace and human response in the life of the spirit, another balance which Augustine did not succeed in maintaining.

The Middle Ages saw the first great flowering of natural theology. Its mode was largely the appeal to reason, its purest form the ontological argument of St Anselm. The latter offers the dazzling prospect of Something for nothing, the deduction of the existence of God (defined as 'that than which no greater can be conceived') simply from an analysis of the implications of that definition. The claim is that what exists is greater than what does not exist so that such a being must, in order to attain his maximal status, include existence among his attributes. One's instinct that this is too clever to be true was confirmed when Kant pointed out the illegitimacy of treating existence as a defining predicate. Its logical status is quite different, namely the assertion that there is an instance of what is defined by the true predicates (in this case, the predicates of omnipotence, omniscience, etc). Thus the ontological argument fails in its logically coercive intent. The existence of God cannot be smuggled into the divine definition and so it remains a logically open question. This conclusion survives ingenious attempts to get round it by claiming that aseity (that is to say, the property of *necessary* being as opposed to merely contingent being) *is* a predicate required for maximal status. There is a distinction to be maintained between internal logical necessity, given a definition, and actual necessity (that is, necessity of an instance of the definition). If 'that than which no greater can be conceived' rightly has aseity among his attributes all that enables us impeccably to deduce is that if there is a God then he exists, in the same way that we can deduce that there are numbers greater than 999 if we accept Peano's axioms for arithmetic. But, just as we can conceive of mathematical systems with a limited number of integers,[24] so we can conceive of worlds in which God does not exist without committing any logical impropriety.[25] Atheism is not an incoherent possibility.

St Thomas Aquinas never accepted Anselm's reasoning. However in the Five Ways[26] he sets out his own natural arguments for the existence of God. They are less austerely abstract than Anselm's, for they take account of certain facts about the world and are not exclusively logical in character. However the facts appealed to are mostly very general, such as the existence of the world and of change within it, so that the emphasis is still very much on the exercise of reason. In summary we might say that the Five Ways appeal to (1) the existence of change so as to conclude that there has to be a first originator of change; (2) the existence of causation so as to conclude that there has to be a first cause; (3) the existence of coming to be and ceasing to be so as to conclude that the world's actual continuance requires an unchanging ground of its existence; (4) the existence of gradations of qualities so as to conclude that there has to be one whose perfection is the ground of all partial qualities; (5) the existence of purpose in the world so as to conclude the necessity of an intelligence directing it. In each case the conclusion leads to the postulation of a being of whom it can be said 'and all understand that this is God'. Only the last of the Five Ways appeals to a rather specific aspect of the world.

The Five Ways are variations on two grand themes of argument for God's existence, namely the cosmological theme (the fact of the world requires an explanation: as Leibniz's great question puts it, Why does something exist rather than nothing?) and the theme of design (the pattern and process of the world exhibits a fruitfulness which speaks of purpose rather than blind chance). In terms of intellectual compulsion the Five Ways are no more coercive than the ontological argument. Hume was to have a lot of shrewd fun at their expense. Of course there has to be some rock-bottom starting point in our account of the world but 'why may not the material universe be the necessary existent . . . for aught we can affirm it [matter] may contain some qualities which, were they known, would make non-existence appear as great a contradiction as that twice two is five.'[27] Physics has explored the possibility of a self-sustaining role for matter in a way that escaped the notice even of Hume's audacious intellect. This is the notion of the bootstrap,[28] a self-consciously constructed counter to the orthodox physical view that matter is composed of identifiable constituents. To the bootstrapper there are no basic elementary particles; rather everything is made out of everything else. That breathtaking possibility – that the world has lifted itself into existence by its own bootstraps, so to speak – is conceivable in modern physics where particles are made out of other particles by a force holding them together and where that force is itself due to the exchange of particles between particles. This double role of particles – as carriers of force and as consequences of force – enables us to think of the possibility of particles making themselves out of themselves in a recursively self-consistent way which identifies carrier and consequence. One of the proponents of this idea, Geoffrey Chew, rather charmingly called it 'nuclear democracy' – nothing is more elementary than anything else.

The bootstrap enables us to think of such a possibility; but I must add that no one has ever succeeded in constructing a theory which did more than approximate in a crude and unsatisfactory way to the idea. Moreover there is good reason to believe that there is an élite of elementary particles, the quarks and the gluons, out of which matter is in fact constructed, rather than a democratic egalitarianism holding sway. As a physically realized idea, therefore, the bootstrap seems dead – but as an enlarger of the intellectual imagination it continues to tease our thoughts. It also serves to contradict the assertion of the classical logicians that cause and effect must be distinct from each other.

As for Hume's views on design, he points out that the perfection of the world is very questionable: 'This world for aught [one] knows is very faulty and imperfect, compared to a superior standard, and was

10

only the first rude essay of some infant deity.'[29] One must acknowledge that the world often presents an ambiguous face when we seek in it to discern signs of benevolent design. Religious believers are sometimes prone to take too facile a view of its perfection. Many years ago there were two sets of films in circulation concerned with the character of the living world. One set, made by the Moody Institute of Science as items of Christian apologetic, concentrated on comfortable aspects of the remarkable way in which life is adapted to its environment. The other set, made by the Disney Organisation without any metaphysical axe to grind, whilst not oblivious of the benevolent side of nature portrayed also its more ruthless aspect. The roles of predators and disease were not overlooked. That would have come as no shock to the biblical writers. The psalmists, in particular, are open to the whole range of experience:

> The young lions roar for their prey,
> seeking their food from God.[30]

> For my loins are filled with burning,
> and there is no soundness in my flesh.
> I am utterly spent and crushed;
> I groan because of the tumult of my heart.[31]

Continued sifting of the arguments from both existence and design has confirmed their shakiness in regard to proof.[32] However that should occasion neither surprise nor dismay. Outside of mathematics there is very little which enjoys such an incontrovertible degree of certainty (and even there Gödel's theorem indicates that an act of faith is necessary concerning the consistency of the system being considered). There is no infallible way of demonstrating the error of the man who claims that the world came into existence five minutes ago. He is logically invulnerable in his preposterous position, and much good may it do him! Whatever Aquinas himself may have thought to be the character of his arguments, their true nature is not that of knock-down demonstration. It is something subtler than that.

Commentators on Aquinas agree that, when he speaks of a 'first' cause, and so on, his concern is with logical hierarchy rather than temporal priority. It is not that God is an originating cause in the remote past (like the fiery explosion of the big bang in physical cosmology) but that he is the fundamental cause in and of the present. In other words, the search for a first cause is a search for the deepest possible understanding of what comes to be, as it comes to be, and a similar search for understanding can be said to characterize the rest of the Five Ways. They are pointers to the divine as the only totally adequate ground of intelligibility. Aquinas's rejection of the possibility of an infinite regress – so strange to us who think naturally of infinite series – is the assertion that there is an attainable comprehensible understanding of all that is. If that is so it would not seem inappropriate that all should 'understand that this is God'. Thus conceived, the aim of natural theology is not demonstration of the divine beyond a peradventure, but rather an understanding of the world through and through, at the most profound level of explanation. The themes of cosmology and design are not proofs but insights.

Perhaps the unconscious recognition of natural theology as a search for understanding is why its second great flowering could occur in the late eighteenth and early nineteenth centuries, despite the severe contemporary criticisms of Hume and Kant. This movement had the character of a whole-hearted appeal to the inspection of the world, in particular to the evidence of design which its intricate and marvellously apt structure was held to reveal. Its leading figure was Archdeacon Paley whose *Evidences* was long considered the outstanding English work of apologetic for theism. A later manifestation was provided by the *Bridgewater Treatises*, founded by a bequest by the eighth Earl of Bridgewater for books devoted to exhibiting 'the Power, Wisdom and Goodness of God, as manifested in the Creation', and with titles such as *The Hand, as Evincing Design*. After all, the fitness of men and animals for life in their environments is a very striking feature of the world which certainly cries out for explanation. Whatever logical cavilling might come from the philosophers, the apparent signs of widespread design were persuasive of the need for a Designer. The precariousness of the quest for insight, arising from our limited powers of imagination of how things can come to be, was never more remarkably illustrated than when Darwin proposed an alternative mechanism, whereby the differential selection of random variations, effected by means of the struggle for survival, could lead to the appearance of design without the need for the intervention of a Designer. It was the offering of an alternative insight, rather than detailed philosophical criticism, which dealt a mortal blow to the natural theology of that day. Natural selection made sense, in broad terms, of the fossil record and also of the existence of small differences between species in mutually isolated environments, such as the different types of finch found in the separate islands of the Galapagos archipelago, which otherwise would seem to be acts of superabundant prodigality if they were special creations of the Creator.

The subsequent advance of knowledge has made less and less plausible the invocation of 'the God of the Gaps', that shadowy deity whose only role was to explain the currently scientifically inexplicable. There are certainly many things that we do not understand. There is no agreement about whether the development of life is straightforwardly to be expected given the right conditions of chemical environment, temperature and radiation,[33] or whether it is so unlikely that we must invoke the rather desperate remedy of supposing it to have arrived on Earth from somewhere else (what one might call 'the Space Being of the Gaps' theory of Francis Crick).[34] The evolution of the eye, which caused Charles Darwin such anxiety, is still mysterious. Yet we have no reason to think that these scientifically stateable questions will not prove in the end to have scientifically stateable answers, however hard they may be to find and by however much they may turn out to require more knowledge than we have at our present disposal.

The God of the Gaps is dead and with him has died the old-style natural theology of Paley and the *Bridgewater Treatises*. No theologian need weep for them, for the God of the Gaps, hovering at the periphery of the known world, was far from being someone of whom it could be said that 'all understand that this is God'. He was proposed as a sort of demiurge, a cause among the other competing causes of the world. When Aquinas spoke of God as 'first cause' he did not consider him thus as a jostling participant among the many efficient causes of the cosmic process. Rather, he is the ground of all that is in the world and not to be identified with any part of its process. He is the author and producer of the play, not a particularly striking actor upon the stage.

Torrance has made the interesting observation that the two great periods of natural theology's flourishing were also periods characterized by strongly dualistic thought about the world.[35] The Middle Ages discriminated between the sensible world of brute perception and the intelligible world of spiritual apprehension. They drew a line between nature and supernature. In the eighteenth century Cartesian dualism proclaimed a division between the extended substance of matter and the thinking substance of mind, whilst the deists sharply differentiated a detached God from the world that he had launched upon its way. The appeal of natural theology in both of these ages lay in its ability to act as a logical bridge across the imposed gulf. It provided a way from one side to the other, as the grand scheme of the *Summa Theologiae* clearly illustrates.

Torrance emphatically rejects this idea that natural theology is just a prior preparation for revealed theology, a warming-up exercise before the real action starts. Rather it is an integral part of the whole theological endeavour:

> If we reject a deistic disjunction between God and the world, which we are bound to do, natural theology cannot be pursued in its traditional abstractive form, as a prior conceptual system on its own, but must be brought within the body of positive theology and be pursued in indissoluble unity with it. No longer extrinsic but intrinsic to the knowledge of God, it will function as a necessary *infra-structure* of theological science.[36]

He calls natural theology the 'epistemological "geometry" ' of revealed theology. In that somewhat curious phrase he has in mind the analogy of the integration of geometry and mechanics which Einstein's General Theory of Relativity brought about. The classical Newtonian view of the question was that space was the given container in which particles of matter executed their mechanical interactions. On this view geometry was a priori to physics. It described the stage on which the dynamical play was to be performed. Just as the scene setters in a theatre can get on with their work in the absence of the actors, so geometrical thought was capable of being pursued in isolation from the consideration of the mechanics of matter. Euclid had his job to do, which Newton could then take over for his purposes.

In General Relativity this is not the case. Space and matter, geometry and physics, impinge upon each other. What we think of as the force of gravity is due to the curvature of space, which is itself due to the distribution of matter. While it may at times be profitable to concentrate one's attention on geometry and at times on matter, one is always conscious that they together form an integrated whole. It is

Torrance's contention that the same is true of natural and revealed theology. His view is congenial to those of us who believe in the unity of knowledge and who consequently think that theology must take account of all that we know about the world in the course of its inquiry. It is also consonant with the history of thought, for when we are seeking an understanding through and through, areas of experience interact with each other and place mutual limitations on the interpretations which are conceivable. One has only to think of the modification of the tone of theological discourse which resulted from the transition from the three-decker universe of the world of antiquity to the vast universe discerned by modern cosmology, to get the point. Taking a contrary position is to risk relegating theology to an intellectual ghetto. Pannenberg has warned of the 'danger of distorting the historical revelation into a gnostic knowledge of secrets' which follows from an 'understanding that puts revelation in contrast to, or even in conflict with, natural knowledge'.[37]

On this view natural theology is an essential study, not just an optional extra for those so inclined. The Darwinian débâcle has had the effect of largely discrediting its pursuit for a century. Nevertheless it is undergoing a welcome revival in our own time. This is occurring not so much at the hands of the theologians (whose nerve, with some honourable exceptions, has not yet returned) but at the hands of the scientists. There has grown up a widespread feeling, especially among those who study fundamental physics, that there is more to the world than meets the eye. Science seems to throw up questions which point beyond itself and transcend its power to answer. They arise from recognizing the potentiality inherent in the structure of the world, its interlocking tightly-knit character, and, indeed, its very intelligibility which makes it open to our inquiry. Thus a physicist such as Paul Davies, who is notably unsympathetic to conventional religion, can nevertheless write, 'It may be bizarre but in my opinion science offers a surer road to God than religion.'[38] We are concerned not only with a revived natural theology but also with a *revised* natural theology. It points to law and circumstance (the assumed *data* of science and so not open to scientific inquiry) rather than to particular occurrences (such as the coming-to-be of life or of the eye). These latter questions are legitimate subjects for scientific investigation and the attempt to capture them for theology is just the error of the God of the Gaps. On the other hand, the former matters of law and circumstance are part of the founding faith of science which it has to assume as the basis of its inquiry. They bring us back to the themes of cosmology and design, pursued at a deeper level than the scientific, in a search for the fullest possible understanding of the world.[39] The insights thus obtained must find their integration within the totality of theological thinking. These are the tasks to which we must address ourselves in the chapters that follow. The purpose of this chapter has been to show that this intellectual quest is a continuation of a long and fruitful tradition of religious thought.

2

Insightful Inquiry

One of the most powerful human motivations is the need we feel to make sense of our experience, to gain a coherent and satisfying understanding of the world in which we live. It is a quest which unites science and theology in comradely concern, for they are both attempting to explore aspects of the way things are.

That quest will not succeed without a commitment to belief and an openness to its correction. The flux of experience has to be interrogated from a point of view which enables us to select the significant in terms of a tentative order. Many men had seen apples fall from trees. Only to a man concerned with the possibility of a general law of gravitational attraction did it occur to ask if that falling might be a manifestation of the same force that kept the Moon in its orbit around the Earth. Yet Newton's insight had to be tested against further investigation of the world. The inaccurate value then believed for the radius of the Earth did not at first permit a perfect reconciliation of the Moon's motion with the behaviour of bodies falling at the Earth's surface, if both were to be described by an inverse square law of gravity. Even when that discrepancy was put right a further difficulty remained, this time in terms of an insufficient understanding of the implications of the idea being developed. Only when Newton was certain that he was right to assume that a spherical body like the Earth would behave gravitationally as if all its mass were concentrated at its centre was he able to publish his great theory. By that time he had come to a realization of how truly universal a phenomenon gravity was. To us, with all the illumination that hindsight brings, it seems strange that he hesitated for a while to apply the gravitational theory, so successful in describing the motions of the planets, also to give an understanding of the way comets behaved in their encounter with the solar system.[1] In that little story we find four elements which characterize all engagement in the search for understanding: (1) the adoption of a belief; (2) its interaction with experience; (3) its fuller conceptual exploration; (4) its generalization to the widest possible range of experience.

It is the search for understanding which inspires the scientist to undertake the prosecution of his research. The occasional moment of resulting illumination is the pay-off which makes worth while all the weary labour and frustration inevitably involved in that endeavour. However much the positivists may tell him that he is simply seeking the harmonious reconciliation of sense experiences or the instrumentalists assure him that it is the power to manipulate phenomena which should be sufficient reward, he knows that they are only tendering him an impoverished and inadequate account of his doings. They offer him a philosophical stone whilst it is the bread of comprehending the pattern and structure of the physical world that he is seeking. As I write several groups of physicists are investigating certain rare events taking place in large experimental arrays deep underground, with many thousands of feet of rock above them to shield the experiments from the unwanted intervention of stray cosmic rays. Is their aim to tell a pretty story about the occasional scintillations they observe? Or to gain some manipulative ability in relation to slabs of material at the bottom of a deep gold mine? Of course not. They are hoping to determine whether, as some physicists have suggested, the proton is not a completely stable particle but very very occasionally decays into lighter particles. Their results will add to our knowledge of what *is*. That potential knowledge gains a significance and interest, justifying the expenditure of money and effort involved, because such an instability, if detected, would encourage the belief, now held by many, that there is a grand unified theory (a GUT for short) which unites three of the four fundamental forces of nature. GUTs offer the possibility of a deeper and more general understanding of fundamental physics than we have achieved hitherto.

Whatever the eventual fate of that particular investigation, this century has already seen an impressive advance in our understanding of the structure of matter. At its beginning there were still some physicists of repute who were sceptical about the actual existence of atoms. By the time I became a research student in 1952 atoms were already 'large' systems from the point of view of elementary particle physics and it was the protons and neutrons forming the constituents of atomic nuclei which were objects of intense study. During my professional lifetime a further revolution has taken place in our understanding. Protons and neutrons themselves are now considered composite, with the quarks and gluons their constituents. There are rather a lot of different quarks[2] and people are beginning to wonder if . . . Thus the relentless search for an understanding of the structure of matter continues.

It is one's scientific instinct to seek for the fullest possible understanding of what is going on. I have already said that within the sphere of scientifically posable questions we have no reason to think that such a pursuit will not yield scientifically stateable answers. Science achieves its success by restricting itself to a certain impersonal mode of inquiry. Its power lies in its ability to interrogate and manipulate the phenomena. Even observational sciences, such as cosmology or evolutionary biology, depend heavily upon the results of experimental sciences, such as physics or genetics, for their capacity to interpret the data.

In the intellectual world nothing comes from nothing; every discipline has its foundational assumptions providing the platform upon which it erects its edifice of understanding. Science assumes the intelligibility of the world, that it is open to our rational inquiry. It then seeks to explain the discerned regularities of the world in terms of the outworking of the basic laws which govern the phenomena. These laws are science's given, in the sense that their form (for instance, an inverse square law of gravitation) and the constants of nature specifying the strengths and balances within them (such as the gravitational constant, fixing the magnitude of the gravitational force between two given masses) are read out from nature. These provide the *data* in terms of which science then attempts to answer the question How? posed in relation to the processes of the world. Of course the modern form of the answer to that question is much subtler than the rigidly mechanical view of the nineteenth century. The clear and determinate world of Newton and Maxwell has dissolved at its constituent roots into the cloudy and fitful world of quantum theory.[3] All the same, the world remains a cosmos whose orderly pattern we can study and admire. Two of the founders of quantum theory were Dirac and Schrödinger. Dirac once spoke of their similarity in outlook, saying:

It was a sort of act of faith with us that any equations which describe fundamental laws of Nature must have great mathematical beauty in them. It was a very profitable religion to hold and can be considered as the basis of much of our success.[4]

Those imbued with a thirst for understanding will not find that science alone will quench it. Not only is there the teeming chaotic fertile world of personal experience, which the cold clear lunar landscape of science, populated by metastable replicating systems but with no people in it, so signally fails to describe. (Who thinks of himself as a collection of quarks, gluons and electrons?) There is also the founding faith that science depends upon, the *data* which themselves call irresistibly for deeper explanation. That the world is intelligible is surely a non-trivial fact about it and the basic laws and circumstance of the universe exhibit a delicate balance which seems necessary if its processes are to evolve such complex and interesting systems as you and me. It is surely inevitable to inquire if these facts are capable of a more profound comprehension than simply the statement that they are the case. If that further understanding is to be had it will be beyond the power of science to provide it. Let us consider these issues in a little more detail.

We are so familiar with the fact that we can understand the world that most of the time we take it for granted. It is what makes science possible. Yet it could have been otherwise. The universe might have been a disorderly chaos rather than an orderly cosmos. Or it might have had a rationality which was inaccessible to us. Suppose we were only able to conceive of things in geometrical terms so that the analytic rationality of the calculus would have been for ever beyond our grasp. Then the circle would have seemed the perfect mode of explanation and our search for an understanding of the solar system would have been condemned to an endless proliferation of epicycle upon epicycle (whether Ptolemaic or Copernican in character) and the beautiful simplicity of the inverse square law would eternally have eluded us. It has not proved so. Our minds have shown themselves to be apt and adequate for the solution of all the problems which the physical world presents to us. Even so grave a threat to intellectual coherence as must have seemed to be posed by the wave/particle duality of light was triumphantly overcome by the invention by Dirac of quantum field theory, which achieved that unpicturable synthesis without a taint of paradox. There is a congruence between our minds and the universe, between the rationality experienced within and the rationality observed without. This extends not only to the mathematical articulation of fundamental theory but also to all those tacit acts of judgement, exercised with intuitive skill, which are equally indispensable to the scientific endeavour.[5] That is too profound a fact to yield to superficial discussion. 'Evolution' can always facilely be invoked as the inexplicable explanation of what is found humanly to be the case. However it seems incredible that, say, Einstein's ability to conceive of the General Theory of Relativity was just a spin-off from the struggle for survival. What survival value does such an ability possess? As Sherlock Holmes said of the practical value of such abstract knowledge, 'You say we go round the sun. If we went round the moon it would not make a pennyworth of difference to me and my work.'[6] Certainly our powers of thought must be in such conformity with the everyday structure of the world that we are able to survive by making sense of our environment. But that does not begin to explain why highly abstract concepts of pure mathematics should fit perfectly with the patterns of the subatomic world of quantum theory or the cosmic world of relativity, both of which are regimes whose understanding is of no practical consequence whatsoever for humankind's ability to have held its own in the evolutionary struggle.

Nor does the fact that we are made of the same stuff (quarks, gluons and electrons) as the universe serve to explain how microcosmic man is capable of understanding the macrocosm of the world. Some fairly desperate attempts have been made along these lines nevertheless, showing how pressing is the need to find an explanation for the significant fact of intelligibility. Speaking of the (dubious) metaphor of the universe as a 'computer' executing a programme specified by the laws of nature, Pagels goes on to say:

> It is fun to explore the metaphor of the universe as a computer and examine what the relation of the cosmic computer is to that other computer, the soft machine inside our head – the brain. The brain is certainly not a digital computer (nor is the universe); but it *is* an organ that transforms information . . . But the brain is a far more complex computer than the macroscopic universe. And it is certainly possible for a complex computer to make a mathematical model of its simplest parts and the rules they obey.[7]

Not only does this go beyond what we presently understand about mind and brain but it also contains no explanatory power. It is simply the bare assertion of the fact that we can understand the world, dressed up in modish jargon. It is rather like the old-style doctors in Molière's parody, ascribing the narcotic properties of opium to its possession of the dormative faculty.

If the deep-seated congruence of the rationality present in our minds with the rationality present in the world is to find a true explanation it must surely lie in some more profound reason which is the ground of both. Such a reason would be provided by the Rationality of the Creator.

The second issue which modern science raises is what we might call the anthropic principle: the fact that a delicate balance seems necessary in the universe's character, similar to that actually found, if the unfolding of its process is to prove capable of evolving systems like ourselves of a complexity sufficient to sustain conscious life. In other words, if you played at Creator and prescribed a universe – twiddled at random the 'cosmic knobs' specifying its nature and structure, so to speak – you would not discover in its subsequent history the fruitfulness actually found in our particular world. Fine tuning of those cosmic knobs is necessary to make men.

We need not recapitulate the many interlocking considerations which have led scientists to that conclusion.[8] It is possible that the ncessary balances involve both law (that is, the pattern and strength of the fundamental forces of nature) and also circumstance (such as the particular way in which the world sprang forth from the fiery singularity of the big bang some fifteen thousand million years ago). Because of very subtle effects which may have been present in the earliest fractions of a second of the universe's history, when there were cosmic regimes of very high energy, remote from our direct experience but not beyond the reach of speculative conjecture, it is not easy to distinguish between what might have been part of the defining initial conditions of our universe (circumstance) and what might have been due to the rapid effect of remarkable processes then occurring (law). For example, we know that there has to have been a very close balance between the competing effects of explosive expansion and gravitational contraction which, at the very earliest epoch about which we can even pretend to speak (called the Planck time, 10^{-43} sec. after the big bang), would have corresponded to the incredible degree of accuracy represented by a deviation in their ratio from unity by only one part in 10^{60}. Had that balance tilted a little more in the direction of expansion, then matter would have flown apart so fast that a world would have resulted too dilute for anything interesting to happen in it. On the other hand, had the balance tilted a little more in the direction of contraction then the world would have collapsed in again upon itself before we had time to appear upon its scene. It may be, however, that this close balance did not have to be written into the universe's initial conditions but was achieved by an ingenious, if highly speculative, process proposed by Alan Guth.[9] He calls it inflation. It is a sort of boiling of space, blowing up the world with exponential rapidity while it lasts. Whatever may be the truth of that, inflation is itself only a realizable possibility if the basic laws of physics conform to a certain kind of pattern. Thus there still has to be something special about a world of anthropic possibility.

Most would agree with Paul Davies when he says about these matters, 'the fact that these relations are necessary for our existence is one of the most fascinating discoveries of modern science'.[10] It seems natural to ask if it is just our luck that things are this way or is there an explanation of them? Science itself cannot explain its own basic laws but scientists have felt uneasy about leaving the matter there. Some have been prompted to speculation that there might be a great variety of universes on offer, so to speak. If that were so and they all had different settings of the cosmic knobs, then we appear in the one we do because it just happened to have the fine tuning permitting us to do so. This notion can be tricked out in various pseudo-scientific ways[11] but, since we have the experience of one universe only, we have scientific motivation to speak of that alone and all that goes beyond it is, in the strictest sense, metaphysical. An alternative metaphysical idea of coherence and economy would be that there is just one world which is the way it is because it is the creation of a Creator who wills it to be capable of evolving beings who can come to know him.

These considerations can form the basis of a natural theology which is based on the pursuit of a thorough understanding of the intelligible tightly-knit structure of the world that science discerns.[12] Because this approach concentrates on the scientifically given rather than on the scientifically open, it is invulnerable to the charge of being a return to the God of the Gaps. The latter was invoked to 'explain' lacunae in

23

contemporary science which one had no reason to suppose would not be adequately filled in by subsequent scientific inquiry; our concern is with those questions which by their nature science is powerless to discuss, but without answers to which its view of the world remains intellectually incomplete and unsatisfying. However, it is necessary to inquire if there are alternative insights which might provide explanations of equal or greater coherence and persuasiveness than that provided by theism. After all, Paley and his friends seemed to have a good case until Darwin came along and drew the rug from beneath their feet with the alternative hypothesis of evolution through competitive process.

We have already considered a many-worlds explanation of the anthropic principle, which would assert that the observed fruitful balance of the universe is no more surprising than learning that a monkey had typed the first lines of *Hamlet* if one also knew that millions of monkeys had been playing with typewriters for millions of years. However, that proposal has too prodigal and contrived an air about it to prove persuasive.[13]

Another possibility, the exact opposite of the many-worlds idea, would be that in reality there is no freedom to twiddle the cosmic knobs, so that the balance between the forces of nature is the way it is because in fact it could be no other. Such an idea had occurred to the fertile mind of David Hume. He wrote that 'may it not happen that could we penetrate into the intimate nature of bodies we should clearly see why it was absolutely impossible they could ever admit of any other disposition?'[14] This might seem a most unlikely suggestion but some have thought that modern physics might give it some credibility. The combination of quantum theory and relativity produces a theory of great subtlety, with a remarkable degree of interlocking necessary in its structure in order to produce consistency. Our exploration of all the implications of this is still continuing and quantum field theory (which is the mathematical articulation of relativistic quantum theory) is still revealing unexpected properties to its students. This has led some to speculate that if we fully understood the matter we should find that there is only one such theory which is non-trivial and totally consistent. That would then fix the cosmic knobs.

Such speculations go far beyond our present knowledge and they do not, in fact, seem to me to be at all likely. Quantum electrodynamics, which is a highly successful theory describing the behaviour of systems composed of electrons and photons only, appears to be perfectly consistent (at least in terms of renormalized field theory). I do not see why there could not be a world composed solely of photons and electrons, though it would be one of which we could not be members, able to appreciate its elegant economy. At a more technical level one may also note that any theory of the world would be expected to take the form of a spontaneously broken gauge symmetry and there would always be arbitrary features in the way the symmetry breaking was realized, with consequent arbitrariness in the resulting balance of effective forces (see p. 34).

Even if such a speculation did in the end prove correct it would only reduce the second of our natural theological considerations (balance) to the first (intelligibility), since it would have been the necessity for the world to be rationally coherent in its structure which would have ensured its anthropic potentiality, through the supposedly unique theory possessing the property of consistency. That would be a very remarkable fact about the world.

We must go on to ask if there is any alternative explanation of the intelligibility of the world, its transparent rational order. The only candidate that appears to be available is that the order that we find in the world is an order that we in fact impose upon it. Kolakowski sketches an answer that could be made by a devil's advocate in reply to the claim that science leads us to God the Great Mathematician: 'Physics is no doubt a work of the mind', he would agree,

> but it is your mind, not God's . . . We are understandably liable to see certain characteristics in the objects we perceive because these objects have indeed been shaped by our minds; hence we imagine that the world in and of itself operates according to certain differential equations, that it is built on well-defined quantitative relationships, and is governed by purpose. A natural illusion, but an illusion all the same.[15]

It is hard to exaggerate how implausible such a view is. It assumes a strange plasticity in experience which we can mould to our reason-seeking will. The feel of scientific inquiry into the world is entirely different. The phenomena encountered often prove extremely surprising and contrary to our intuition. They resist our attempts to bend them to our prior expectation. How does it come about that there are remarkable changes in our understanding of the physical world, such as resulted when Newtonian mechanics gave way to quantum theory and relativity? Surely they arise as a response to our discernment of what actually is.[16] Those who believe that we impose a structured grid of interpretation on the world in order to cope with the flux of its phenomena have proved singularly inept in demonstrating the nature of this supposedly man-generated order. Kant thought that he had shown the a priori necessity of Euclidean geometry. Since it proves, in fact, just to be one possibility among those actually encountered, he obviously deceived himself. Of course we approach the world from a particular point of view, but it receives its confirmation or necessary correction from interaction with the way things are. We have no reason to suppose that the rationality of the world is a human artefact.

Leibniz's principle of sufficient reason, the search for an explanation through and through, has been our motivation in this discussion. It is a way of thinking that comes naturally to a scientist and we can see it at work in contemporary physics. The desire to unify our understanding of the structure of matter by the successful construction of a GUT (see p. 18), or even more ambitiously (by the incorporation of the fourth fundamental force, gravity) by the construction of theories of supergravity or superstrings, is just such a striving at the scientific level to achieve a deeply-rooted comprehensive rationality. The natural theology with which we are concerned is the attempt to carry this quest to the deepest and most fundamental level possible, to answer the question put by Newton, 'Whence is it that Nature does nothing in vain and whence arises all the Order and Beauty that we see in the World?'[17]

It might be objected that the search for explanation through and through is an illegitimate aspiration. Perhaps there is no achievable fullness of understanding, merely an infinite regress of explanation upon explanation, nesting inside one another like Chinese boxes, just as, perhaps, there are no ultimate constituents of matter but bigger fleas have lesser fleas and so *ad infinitum*. The introduction of God would then simply foreclose the issue by making the Creator a stopper to further inquiry. Mackie wittily says that once God is introduced as a cause then the search for a cause of this cause is out of order and thus 'the theist loses every battle but the last'.[18]

I cannot subscribe, as a principle of method, to such pessimism about the rational comprehension of the world. The question of whether a full understanding can be found is only to be answered by attempting its pursuit. That the foundation of such a pursuit is indeed theism gains credibility from the cumulative case for God's existence,[19] which sees him as providing not only the ground of reason but also of the beauty and moral order of the world and of the religious experience of men within it. Only one who is the ground of all could provide the necessary linkage of these diverse aspects of reality, coincidentally coexisting, which otherwise seem curiously unrelated.

It is also possible, of course, to decline to ask the question altogether. Writing about anthropic considerations Mackie says, 'Atomic and nuclear physics are, no doubt, intricate enough to be of theoretical as well as practical interest, but we cannot see them as involving reciprocal adjustments which might plausibly be taken as signs of purposiveness.'[20] That strikes me as condescending and untrue. He has a better point when he goes on to suggest that if the balance of the laws of nature were different then, while the evolution of life as we know it would have been impossible, perhaps there would have been different potentialities for the organization of matter of an equally 'fruitful' character. Such a suggestion claims substantial intellectual credit for what is not known, but in its nature it is as difficult categorically to deny as to affirm. Frankly we have such a struggle to understand, let alone predict, the behaviour of matter under the laws we know (molecular biology is no trivial discipline) that it is quite beyond us to give a detailed and reliable account of what might happen if those laws were different. We can simply say two things, one general, the other more specific. In general terms it seems clear that for fruitfulness the universe must last a long enough time and not be too dilute. In more specific terms the evolution of carbon-based life (the only fruitful system of which we have certain knowledge) undoubtedly calls for delicate balance in the working of the world. If alternative settings of the cosmic knobs did indeed lead to complex 'conscious' systems, that would again be a very remarkable property of intelligible worlds.

These anthropic considerations are examples of what Bartholomew somewhat ironically calls 'the *significance test* approach to theism', for they bear an analogy to procedures used by statisticians to test hypotheses. Summarizing the argument he writes:

Let us set up the hypothesis that there is no directing purpose behind the universe so that all change and development is the product of 'blind chance'. We then proceed to calculate the probability that the world (or that aspect of it under consideration) would turn out as we find it. If that probability turns out to be extremely small we argue that the occurrence of something so rare is totally implausible and hence that the hypothesis on which it is calculated is almost certainly false. The only reasonable alternative open to us is to postulate a grand intelligence to account for what has occurred. This procedure is based on the logical disjunction *either* an extremely rare event has occurred *or* the hypothesis on which the probability is calculated is false. Faced with this choice the rational thing to do is to prefer the latter alternative.[21]

We must acknowledge that there are a number of difficulties in such an approach. One is that it involves a dialogue between probability and interpretation. For any really complex system any particular state of its existence will be highly improbable since it is selected from a vast range of alternative possibilities. Thus any particular state's occurrence will only be remarkable if that configuration is endowed with specific properties which make it seem of special significance. The point was lucidly made by Michael Polanyi when he discussed an arrangement of small white pebbles laid out by the station master of Abergele and spelling out the message 'Welcome to Wales by British Railways'.[22] Who could doubt that this configuration of stones is rightly to be interpreted as being significant? Yet if one cast the stones at random on the patch of ground and calculated the probability of attaining *that particular arrangement* that resulted, its a priori probability would be the same infinitesimal amount as that for the arrangement conveying the message of welcome. The latter seems significant for us, while the former would not, not simply because of its small probability but also because it is capable of significant interpretation. To get the total meaning of that situation one has to be acquainted with English orthography. Someone ignorant of the language would no doubt perceive an intrinsically orderly pattern but its full meaning would elude him. Thus the coincidences which seem significant and demand explanation will depend upon the interpretative scheme with which we approach the world. That is, of course, just another example of the fact to which we have already alluded, that all our interaction with the world requires the adoption of a point of view, which is capable of subsequent correction if necessary.

Another problem is to make sure that we have calculated the odds in the right way. An hypothesis will always be involved, stating that certain events are truly random, that each of them is as likely to occur as any other. That assumption might be false for reasons we have not taken into account. If you throw a die and it comes up a six ten times in succession, if I think the die is true I shall be very surprised, for the probability of that happening is 1.65×10^{-8}. However it is always possible that you are using a loaded die and I have just misunderstood the situation. This caveat applies particularly to those who (declining our warning to confine themselves to law and circumstance and avoid discussion of specific occurrences in the process of the world) seek to make a case for something like theism by purportedly showing, say, that the coming-to-be of life is so fantastically improbable an event that there must be an Intelligence at work to bring it about. When someone like Fred Hoyle calculates the chance of a protein forming in the amino acid soup of early Earth as being the same as solving the Rubik cube blindfold,[23] he is assuming that the amino acids would arrange themselves into a chain in a random sequence, like stringing beads on a string. However it is surely more probable that there are biochemical pathways, constructing chains from sub-chains and so on, which make that picture inappropriate. The odds need to be calculated on a more informed basis.

A special problem arises when one attempts, as our discussion has done, to consider the 'significance test approach to theism' in relation to the character of the universe itself. What probability can one assign to the uniquely one-off? We normally calculate probabilities by analysing the range of alternatives but we do not have experience of other universes, if such there be. If there were only one possible setting of the cosmic knobs then one would think very differently about the problem than if there were many.

I do not think that this particular difficulty should cause us to relinquish our intuitive feeling that the balance of the world is significant and requires an explanation which goes beyond the brute assertion that things are the way they are in the one world of which we have experience and there's an end of it. Tennant confidently remarks concerning such an attitude attributing significance 'If teleology strays from the path of logical rectitude into one marked by logicians with a warning post it does so in the lighthearted company of common sense and inductive science.'[24] He speaks of an 'alogical probability which is the ground of life and which has been found to be the ultimate basis of all scientific induction'.[25] That last remark reminds us again of the tacit intuitive skill whose exercise is as essential to scientific inquiry as it is to any other search for understanding of the world. Induction can only be defended by appeal to it.

Thus the anthropic arguments of natural theology, based on law and circumstance, seem to me to survive this discussion of the problems associated with them. It is fair to inquire whether they will also survive the advance of knowledge. They are based on our current understanding of the world and its process. We are only too aware of how greatly that differs from the understanding of a generation or two ago. Is there not the possibility, indeed the probability, that a generation or two into the future it will all look very different again and what will have become of our arguments then? He who marries the scientific spirit of the age has every reason to fear imminent widowerhood and does that not make this sort of natural theology too precarious to be satisfactory? My instinct is to feel that, while correlations in the structure of the world may be revealed to us which are currently hidden and which may explain naturally what now seems to us to be coincidental, there is likely to remain a degree of balance necessary for life and irreducibly given in scientific terms, which will call for a deeper explanation. However that may turn out as cosmology progresses, there is nevertheless no denying that it is to the appeal to the intelligibility of the world that we must turn if we want the argument of natural theology with the greatest degree of fundamentality and the highest prospect of endurance. It is a fact about the world of manifest significance and proven staying power. Torrance says about the universe that science investigates that it 'does have something to "say" to us, simply by being what it is, contingent *and* intelligible in its contingency, for that makes its lack of self-explanation inescapably problematic.'[26] He goes on to speak of the world's 'mute cry for sufficient reason'. St Augustine speaks of our hearts being restless till they find their rest in God. He had in mind principally the longing of love in the depths of our being, but it is also true that our intellectual restlessness will only find its final quiet in the vision of God.

The principal threat to the insight of intelligibility seems to arise from quantum theory. While there is no doubt about how to apply that theory to the calculation of experimental consequences and while these calculations provide a highly successful account of the behaviour of microscopic phenomena, there is still a great deal of unresolved dispute about the interpretation of what is going on and about the nature of the quantum world.[27] The view held by the majority of physicists asserts that there is no cause to be assigned to individual quantum events. It is only the overall statistical character of many events of a similar kind that the theory can predict. If that is right it provides a remarkable stopper, in terms of human knowledge, to the search for an understanding through and through. To say that is not to proclaim quantum events to be totally irrational but simply to note that they have an arational element in their behaviour, within a statistically regular pattern of occurrence. Some have found such a notion unpalatable and have constructed 'hidden variable' theories which assign precise but undiscernible causes to individual quantum events. On that view the statistical character of quantum theory arises from ignorance rather than from principle. Nevertheless such theories have not found wide acceptance among physicists, despite what one might have thought would be their common-sense appeal. The reason for this lack of enthusiasm for hidden variable quantum mechanics is interesting. Partly it is due to technical difficulties in combining such ideas with those of special relativity, but principally it is the result of a feeling that the theories have an unnatural air of contrivance about them. They do not exhibit that economic elegance we have come to expect of fundamental physical theory. Thus one rational principle (simplicity) militates against another rational principle (total explanation).

The moral of this perplexing tale seems to be that there are limits which human rationality may encounter and have to respect in seeking its understanding of the world (of which the reticences of apophatic theology about the nature of God would provide a more striking example) but that is no discouragement to the quest for such thorough understanding as proves accessible to us. Indeed the history of quantum theory is a history of the pursuit of rationality in the strange world of microscopic phenomena. The intelligibility of the world is open to such limitation as the idiosyncrasy of its entities may impose upon us, but it is still a world marvellously transparent to human reason. (Nevertheless there remains a dilemma for theology which Einstein sensed in his famous remark about not believing in a God who played dice. Is God the true hidden variable, determining the physically undetermined? I shall later (p. 58) reject the possibility of that being by itself an adequate mode for characterizing God's interaction with the world, but it might be part of that interaction all the same. Or is the radical indeterminacy of quantum events a physical sign of the freedom given to creation to be itself? I do not know, but my instinct is to incline to the latter point of view.)

The modern philosopher who has made the search for understanding the key to his metaphysical system is the Canadian Jesuit, Bernard Lonergan. His great work, *Insight*, is based on the analysis of, the centrality of, and ultimately the apotheosis of, understanding. God is for him the root explanation of the world that lies open to rational exploration. He writes: 'If the real is completely intelligible, then God exists. But the real is completely intelligible. Therefore God exists.'[28] Natural theology's insight of intelligibility could not be put with greater succinctness and forcefulness. For Lonergan the quest of the intellect is the quest for God, for

> if one is genuine in denouncing obscurantism and in demanding the unconditioned [Lonergan's term for that which is] either one already adores God without naming him or else one has not far to go to reach him . . . God is the unrestricted act of understanding, the eternal rapture glimpsed in every Archimedean cry of Eureka.[29]

That search for the unity of knowledge which inspires the physicist to seek his Grand Unified Theory, if pursued with tenacity eventually leads beyond physics to theology, for 'In spite of the imposing name, "transcendence" is the elementary matter of raising further questions.'[30] St Anselm gave the splendid definition of theology as *fides quaerens intellectum*, faith seeking understanding. Lonergan points us to the other side of the coin: *intellectus quaerens fidem*, understanding in search of faith.

The purpose of this chapter has been to sketch just such a quest. Its pursuit involves at every stage a dialogue between evidence and interpretation, the continuing effort to sift the significant from the merely coincidental. Such activity involves the exercise of imagination as well as analysis, so that it is properly characterized as insightful rather than demonstrative. Its aim is the attainment of a comprehensive rationality within which everything finds its place. Included in that scheme will be a role for the contingent, since it is part of the quiddity of things that some events happen rather than others. Our understanding does not have to be contained solely within a rigid necessity; it can also assign a creative significance to chance. That is an issue which the scientist encounters more in the study of complex physical systems than in the simplicities of fundamental physics. In our next chapter we must give it our consideration.

3

Order and Disorder

Our appeal has been to the order of the world. The regimes of concern to fundamental physics, which are the regimes of the very large (cosmology) and the very small (elementary particle physics), do indeed seem to display a remarkably beautiful structure. The evolution of the universe according to the laws of General Relativity, and the patterns described by particle physics, are sources of considerable intellectual delight to those privileged to study them. The processes described by these two branches of physics are thought to have interacted fruitfully with each other during the era immediately following the big bang.

'The two regimes met in the earliest instants of cosmic history when the whole world was an arena in which the fundamental forces of nature held symmetric sway. For a moment they all acted on an equal footing but as the universe cooled the separate forces we now know (strong, electromagnetic, weak and gravitational) "crystallized out" at their observable strengths through a process called spontaneous symmetry breaking. That is to say, the perfect primeval order was fragmented into the considerable but lesser order that we see today, by effects analogous to the way in which the perfect symmetry of a sphere balanced on the tip of a cone would be broken by the small fluctuation which caused the ball to roll down to the base in some particular direction.'

That is the highly speculative but attractive account offered by those physicists who seek a totally unified theory of the forces of nature and who apply it with unrestricted boldness to speculate on events occurring when the universe was between 10^{-43} and 10^{-10} seconds old.[1] Beautiful as is the order that we now perceive, they believe there was once a golden age when, fleetingly, it was even greater. On this view the disparities now observed between the forces of nature are accidents of their history. These accidents need not have been literally universal. As it cooled and 'crystallized' the universe might have split up into

34

different domains in which the consequent balance between the forces took different forms, just as a ferromagnet whose magnetism has been destroyed by heating can cool into a state in which the restored magnetism acts in different directions in different domains (see p. 46). The inflationary scenario (p. 23) would have pushed the domain walls beyond our ken when space boiled and expanded, so that our particular neck of the cosmic woods looks uniform in its behaviour. Nevertheless, elsewhere, over our horizon, different possibilities are realized. This idea forms the most respectable speculation seeking to explain away the anthropic coincidences. Different domains give different balances and we live in the domain in which they come out right because, once again, we could appear in no other. However, this speculation, even if true, does not seem to me to go the whole way necessary to offer an explanation, since there is still a wide selection of fundamental theories to choose from whose symmetries might spontaneously be broken, and not all these theories would yield universes endowed with anthropic potentiality. Once again one can ask what would be wrong with a universe which was composed simply of photons and electrons? (So it is still a significant fact about the world that the fundamental physical theory that actually occurs is capable of yielding men and women. If the idea of inflated domains is the reason why there is a region where the precise balances resulting from that theory's symmetry breaking lie within anthropic limits, then that could be a gain for the theist, who might be loath to invoke direct divine intervention in the fluctuations triggering the exact form of crystallization of the forces that we see today. Otherwise there would be the danger of a return to the God of the Gaps, the divine participator within physical process. That difficulty does not apply to the concept of the Creator who has ordained the fact, necessarily treated as given by science, that his universe should contain more than photons and electrons. He is simply laying down the conditions which are prior to any physical process.)

This is heady talk, but somewhere in between the fundamental physics of the very large and the very small – lying in fact at about the geometric mean of their length scales – is the world of everyday, described by the sciences of chemistry, biology and anthropology. However symmetric and orderly these extreme worlds may be, the world of everyday – the world, in fact, of our immediate concern as people – seems much more untidy. It is the realm, not only of order, but also of disorder. The cold hard beauty of fundamental physics does not compensate for the dissatisfaction we feel at the surd of suffering which makes itself felt through the imperfections and malfunctions of that physical world of our direct experience. A natural theology which did not speak to that would not prove very persuasive.

The everyday world is constructed out of constituents from the quantum world, but as these entities combine together into systems of greater and greater complexity new possibilities come into being, exhibiting properties (such as life or consciousness) which were unforeseeable in terms of the simpler constituents out of which they are made, whilst only being realizable through the potentialities with which those same entities are endowed. Thus growth in organization produces genuine novelty and each level (biological, human, social) enjoys its own autonomy in terms of concepts which are not simply reducible to those associated with lower levels. So I would wish to say,[2] but there are reductionists who assert the contrary, who can speak of human beings as 'survival machines – robot vehicles blindly programmed to preserve the selfish molecules known as genes'.[3] And, of course, those selfish genes are just bundles of quarks and gluons and electrons, when all's said and done. As soon as the rhetorical dust has settled one is aware of the astonishing implausibility of the claims being made in such grotesque statements. As Keith Ward says of such reductionist thinking: 'The basic intellectual defect with theories of this sort is that they deny the most certain and obvious observable facts and try to replace them with very general, speculative, abstract theory'.[4] In the end rationality itself dissolves away, for if mind is really nothing but the epiphenomenon of brain, then there is no rightness or wrongness in thought; neural events simply happen and that is that.

Such a view is inadequate to describe the world of our experience. Each level of that world enjoys its own rational intelligibility and is open to our understanding on its own terms. As Meynell says, summarizing Lonergan's views on level structure: 'Each level (A) differs from the one directly below it (B) in that what was a merely coincidental manifold at the level of B becomes systematic, or able to be grasped by direct insight, at the level of A.[5] Only if we adopt the categories appropriate to the system's organization will we be able coherently to discern its character. (We totally fail to grasp the nature of man if we regard him as just a genetic survival machine.) Even at the level of chemistry one can find unexpected novelty emerging, as the so-called 'chemical clock' illustrates.[6] This involves a linked series of reactions in which 'red' and 'blue' chemicals, X and Y, are synthesized or broken down through interactions involving other chemicals present in the solution. At fixed concentrations of the latter one might have expected that X and Y would settle down to an equilibrium 'purple' mixture of definite proportions. For some sets of circumstances this is indeed the case, but for others a remarkable rhythmic oscillation is set up, with the system alternating regularly between red and blue like the ticking of a clock. This behaviour involves the collaboration of billions upon billions of molecules, a totally unexpected manifestation of large-scale organization. What seems extraordinary coincidence at the microscopic molecular level is understood at the macroscopic level in terms of the limit cycles of a dissipative system. (Its explanation requires the use of more mathematics than is appropriate here[7] but we may note that the abstract key to this behaviour lies in the non-linear reflexive character of the equations describing the effects of the reactions on the concentrations of X and Y. The mathematical property of non-linearity expresses the fact that doubling a quantity does not produce more of the same but a totally new possibility. Reflexivity is the mathematical property of self-linkage, so that effects, so to speak, bend round upon themselves in a way that has to prove self-consistent. Such self-reference, or recursions as the mathematicians call them, can produce unexpectedly tricky situations. Consider the self-referring proposition in logic: 'This sentence is false'. If it is true it is false; if it is false it is true.)

Even the familiar phenomenon of the flow of time from past to future has the character of an effect of organizational level. The processes of elementary particle physics are almost exactly time-symmetric, that is they make no discrimination between past and future.[8] That fact is in striking contrast to our macroscopic experience that we can recall the past but not foretell the future. The direction of time's arrow is usually explained as being a thermodynamic effect, whose orientation is defined by the increase of entropy for bulk systems. The key idea to hold on to in the discussion that follows is the fact, familiar from the way papers accumulate on our desks, that without external intervention things tend to get more and more higgledy-piggledy as time goes by. It is this transition from order to disorder that indicates the direction in which time is flowing.

Thermodynamics is a subject which began at the beginning of the nineteenth century with Fourier's discovery of the law of heat conduction in bodies. This is a manifestly irreversible, time-directed, process. If an iron bar is hot at one end and cool at the other, it will gradually change its state with time until it attains a uniform temperature throughout. Once this thermal equilibrium is achieved it cannot be reversed if the bar is left undisturbed by external influences. Thus the time-asymmetric science of heat has a different character from the time-symmetrical mechanical science of Newton. The latter sees the world as a perpetual-motion machine, redistributing energy among its parts in the course of their mutual interactions but never losing access to the energy thus exchanged. Its paradigm systems are the steadily oscillating pendulum or the ceaselessly revolving planets. On the other hand the world of thermodynamics is in a constant process of running down; time elapsing leads to decay. Its paradigm system is the heat engine whose boiler has continuously to be fed with fuel to keep it going. Yet Joule's discovery of the conservation of energy and of the mechanical equivalent of heat linked the phenomena and showed that these apparently different world views must be mutually interacting aspects of the one way things are. Scientists from Carnot through Clausius and Kelvin to Boltzmann sought to investigate how irreversibility could enter a world whose constituents were particles obeying reversible Newtonian dynamics. The key lay in the concept of entropy (a measure of the disorder of a system) and the tendency for it to increase during the evolution of isolated systems (the celebrated second law of thermodynamics). Thus entropy became the orienter of evolution, the pointer directing the arrow of time. The role of randomness in the process was made clear when Boltzmann identified the state of maximum entropy of a complex system as the most probable state it could attain. It is only in some sort of shuffling process that such probabilistic properties could assume a significance. Boltzmann sought to identify this shuffling with the effect of particle collisions.

The existence of these 'attractor states' of maximum entropy, towards which thermodynamic systems evolve, shows that for these systems only partial control is possible. Not all final states that are conceivable are attainable. Max Planck put this with striking force when he wrote:

> From this point of view Nature does not permit processes whose final states she finds less attractive than their initial states. Reversible processes are limiting cases. In them Nature has an equal propensity for initial and final states; this is why the passage between them can be made in both directions.[9]

Thus it seems that the way in which mechanics and thermodynamics are compatible is that the role of the latter is to restrict the possibilities which are actually attainable among the range of states which the former permits. Since the final states of one process are the initial states of the next there is a thermodynamically-conditioned historical constraint operating in the evolution of the world. (How this comes about we shall discuss in more detail later; p. 44.) However much the fundamental physicist may wish to frame his understanding in terms of being, the scientist who is describing the processes of the world must also take account of the role of becoming.

The contrast between the fundamental physicist's attitude to time and that of the scientist concerned with macroscopic phenomena can be brought out by comparing statements made by two Nobel prizewinners in these two disciplines. Einstein, in a letter written towards the end of his life, once delivered himself of the astonishing opinion that 'to us convinced physicists the distinction between past, present and future is an illusion, though a persistent one.'[10] He was expressing the God's-eye view of the classical relativist who thinks in terms of the space-time continuum (embracing past, present and future) laid out before him. It is interesting to recall that when Einstein took the first step towards creating the modern science of cosmology by his application of General Relativity to the whole universe, he sought to find a static (that is, an eternally changeless) solution to describe the world. It could only be done by tinkering with the equations.[11] Friedmann and Lemaître subsequently showed that the original undisturbed equations admitted time-dependent solutions corresponding to just such an expanding universe as Hubble's researches later revealed to be the case. It is one of the great discoveries of this century that the universe itself has a history and partakes of becoming.

Although quantum physicists often seem to talk in similarly eternal terms about the world (as, for example, when they think of Feynman diagrams as spread out in an infinite space-time continuum[12]) their stance is modified by the unique and controversial role of measurement in quantum theory. The 'infinite' time in which the virtual interactions of Feynman diagrams appear to take place is in reality the time, finite but very long in relation to the natural timescales of the processes involved, elapsing between successive acts of measurement. Each new act of measurement, by its radically unpredictable outcome, creates a new circumstance. There is, therefore, an intrinsic openness to the future built somewhere into the structure of quantum theory which does not correspond to a similar openness to the past.[13] One sees that most strikingly in the highly controversial (and to me most implausible) many-worlds interpretation proposed for measurement in quantum theory. It states that at each individual act of measurement the universe divides into a series of disjoint universes in each of which one of the possible results of the measurement actually occurs. That process would give an intrinsic direction to time, namely that defined by an ever-increasing multiplicity of independent worlds.

Most physicists find the wanton prodigality of the many-worlds interpretation too distasteful to be convincing. Instead they incline to the idea that it is the intervention of large, effectively classical, laboratory instruments into the measuring process which brings about the obtaining of a particular result on a particular occasion. The Copenhagen interpretation, which Niels Bohr and his friends hammered out in the early days of quantum theory, took such a view. Many of us, while inclining to look in that sort of direction for a solution of the problem, do not find that the orthodox Copenhagen interpretation faces squarely enough the perplexities involved in its adoption. Bohr was quite content to divide the world into a fitful quantum component under observation and a reliable classical component by means of which the observations were made. Such a dualism will not do. Laboratory apparatus is made out of quantum constituents just like everything else. How the determinator emerges from its indeterminate substrate is a pressing problem neglected by Copenhagen orthodoxy. Surely its full understanding will depend upon a proper conception of the role of time for large systems, since it seems likely that it is the *irreversible* registration of results by classical measuring instruments which produces the determinating act.

In contrast to a fundamental physicist like Einstein, a scientist like Prigogine, who is concerned with macroscopic phenomena and whose Nobel prize was awarded for his work on the irreversible thermo-dynamics of systems far from equilibrium, takes a view of time which is in accord with the commonsense experience that it has a direction. He relates the existence of the arrow of time to the existence of systems of a complexity sufficient to include an element of randomness in their description. In his book with Stengers they write:

> Only when a system behaves in a sufficiently random way may the difference between past and future, and therefore irreversibility, enter into its description . . . The arrow of time is the manifestation of the fact that the future is not given, that, as the French poet Paul Valéry emphasized, 'time is a construction'.[14]

The way that an element of randomness is seen to create openness to the future assigns a more positive role to chance in the process of the world than is acknowledged by those like Monod[15] who see its operation as destructive of all significance.

The physical world is thus characterized at its different levels both by the timeless order of which Einstein speaks and also by the evolving process of which Prigogine speaks, in which randomness has its part to play. It is a world of being and becoming. Prigogine and Stengers refer to this recent scientific recognition as 'the reconceptualization of physics . . . We see now that there is a more subtle form of reality involving both time and eternity'.[16] That may be a recent realization for modern physics but it is one with which other disciplines have been acquainted for a long while. We recall the use by the Fathers of the idea of the *Logos* (p. 7). Torrance says that 'It is to patristic thought that we owe the conception of an ontology in which structure and movement, the noetic and the dynamic, are integrated in the real world.'[17] The ideas of being and becoming have a long intellectual history. Their coexistence means that at any given time there is both a clarity and an opacity in our understanding of the world. What things will be is not completely manifested in what they presently are. The acceptance by science of an essential role for time makes its world-view more open and more readily reconcilable with human experience than would be the case if the austere and timeless perspective of fundamental physics were its only insight.

The matter which is of the most immediate concern to our present discussion is the role of randomness in the processes of the world. It manifests itself in a variety of ways. Its most radical form is the irreducibly chance happenings of individual quantum events, that 'playing at dice' by God that Einstein instinctively disliked so much. This only directly effects systems which are microscopic (technically, whose action is of the order of magnitude of Planck's constant). Only in exceptional circumstances will events at that level have effects which are amplified sufficiently to impinge on the world of everyday occurrence. Typically it is the case that quantum fluctuations of the individual constituents cancel each other out when added together, so that macroscopic systems exhibit behaviour with a sufficient degree of determinism to satisfy Newton. Indeed his mechanics remains perfectly adequate to describe dynamics at the macroscopic level, needing only to be modified if velocities of the order of magnitude of the velocity of light are involved, in which case the equally deterministic dynamics of Special Relativity must be employed. Yet even the deterministic character of classical mechanics does not produce so tightly-ordered a world as one might have supposed.[18] This is because of instabilities present in even quite simple systems. The exploration of this idea will make demands on the non-scientific reader. He should bear in mind that what is being discussed is an unexpected sensitivity of the mechanical world to the effects of fine differences. The very simple systems that the pioneers of dynamics investigated, and which remain the standard fodder for students, have a robustness about them which means that small changes in circumstances produce only small changes in consequences. It turns out that this is an untypical behaviour. Most dynamical systems exhibit a surprisingly unstable response to small variations. There is a kind of fragility about them which limits our ability to predict and control them. Indeed, the modern study of such instabilities has been given the name 'chaos'.

As an example, consider elastic collisions of a small sphere with an array of large fixed spheres. Without doubt this is a system to which Newton's laws apply in their full rigour. Each trajectory is perfectly determinate. However, small variations in the initial direction of motion of the small sphere produce cumulatively larger and larger differences in the directions of rebound after successive collisions with the fixed spheres. Consequently a small uncertainty about the initial direction in which the small sphere is moving rapidly makes it impossible to predict which of the large spheres it will collide with in the course of its motion. In terms of effectively attainable knowledge, the system's behaviour contains a large element of randomness. It is a similar sensitivity to small details of throwing that makes us attribute the fall of a die to 'chance'. Laplace had spoken of a demonic calculator who, given the positions and momenta of all the particles in a Newtonian world, could predict that world's future and retrodict its past, so that effectively all time was present to him in that instant of knowledge. That chilling thought is the claim of mechanical physics to enjoy an eternal viewpoint. The claim dissolves away in the face of the fuzziness of strongly unstable dynamical systems.[19] As Prigogine and Stengers say 'when faced with these unstable systems Laplace's demon is just as powerless as we'.[20] The apparently deterministic proves to be intrinsically unpredictable. It is suggested that the natural interpretation of this exquisite sensitivity is to treat it, not merely as an epistemological barrier, but as an indication of the ontological openness of the world of complex dynamical systems. Such a view is congenial to the critical realist for whom epistemology and ontology are always closely linked.

The simplest instabilities are bifurcations, points at which alternative paths of evolution are open to a dynamical system. As an elementary example consider a bead threaded on a smooth wire which has the shape of an inverted U. The slightest perturbation can cause it to slide down on one side or the other, with two totally different motions resulting, depending upon which side is thus selected. At such points of bifurcation the system is extremely sensitive to its interaction with the environment. If a gentle breeze were blowing from left to right than it would be more likely that the bead would execute the motion on the right hand side of the U. Points of instability are circumstances in which it is not possible satisfactorily to treat the system as isolated from the effects of its surroundings.

The instabilities of complex dynamical systems produce a degree of intrinsic randomness which goes beyond mere subjective ignorance on our part of their precise states of motion. We discussed earlier the scattering of a small sphere by a set of fixed large spheres. If a beam of small spheres is fired at the fixed spheres it will get diffused by the subsequent collisions in a way that cannot be controlled however tightly we try to collimate the initial beam. (A physicist, in a technical aside, would say that a region of initial phase space, however small, will spread throughout a large region of phase space by filamentary diffusion. Its total volume is preserved, as Liouville's theorem requires, but it is dispersed to become dense throughout phase space. In other words, motions which start arbitrarily close to each other can ultimately end up arbitrarily far apart.) That uncontrollable diffusion is what we have called an intrinsic randomness. Its unfolding consequence produces an irreversibility which defines a direction of time. It is the direction of increasing dispersion of the system, or increasing entropy.

Suppose we had taken a film of that beam of small spheres undergoing its scattering. Now let us run the film backwards. We would appear to start with a ragged state of motion, with small spheres moving in all directions. Miraculously this would sort itself out as the film ran on its backward way, with the small spheres coming together to emerge as a neatly collimated beam. Such a sequence would be a transition from disorder to order, the reverse of what thermodynamics alleges to be possible. The reversed film certainly portrays a *dynamically* possible motion, since it corresponds to what we would actually obtain if we reversed the spheres' velocities at some instant in the original motion. By that act of reversal we should have created a state of motion in which all the small spheres' positions and velocities were so cleverly correlated as to produce the final emerging beam. The statement of the second law of thermodynamics is that such delicately correlated initial states are not accessible to us in the world as we find it. They are divided, in fact, from the states we do have at our disposal by an infinite entropy barrier. Thus, as we said earlier, thermodynamics acts as a constraint upon dynamics, by prescribing the possible initial circumstances from which our experience derives.

While the second law of thermodynamics proclaims that change and decay in all around we see, we are also aware of systems which seem to be swimming against the tide of increasing entropy. They develop and maintain an order, in contrast to the increasing disorder around them. We ourselves are examples of such systems, as we maintain in being

44

the intricate patterns of our bodies. The fact is that in appropriate circumstances the instabilities of dynamical systems can actually prove the triggers of order rather than chaos. This is made clear by the study of what are called dissipative systems.[21] These are systems far from equilibrium requiring a source of energy to keep them in being. (Hence the adjective 'dissipative'.) The chemical clock (p. 37) is an example. Another is provided by the hydrodynamical phenomenon of Bénard instability. Fluid is contained between two horizontal plates and the lower plate is heated. A temperature gradient is thereby set up in the fluid. At low values of the temperature difference between the two plates the heat flow proceeds by conduction. Above a certain threshold of temperature gradient, however, an instability sets in and the heat transfer becomes convective, that is it is conveyed by the bulk motion of the fluid. This motion is far from chaotic for it is organized within vertical hexagonal columns, or convective cells, of a characteristic size. Once again, as with the chemical clock, an effect is produced involving the collaborative behaviour of billions upon billions of molecules. This orderly phenomenon runs counter to one's naive expectation that everything would just become more and more higgledy-piggledy. If you are worried about how this squares with the second law, let me point out that a dissipative system, because of its source of energy input, is not an isolated system. It is therefore able to get rid of entropy by exporting it into the environment. The internal order is produced at the expense of external disorder and overall there is an entropy increase. The marvellous order of living beings is brought about in a similar way.

In situations of instability it is small fluctuations which trigger the generation of unexpected order. Interesting analogies occur in biology. The large pillars of earth which form the nests of termites are examples of apparent collaborative activity in the insect world. The first stage of their construction is a scurrying of termites dropping little lumps of earth at random. Each lump is impregnated with a hormone which attracts other termites. By chance a few more lumps are deposited in one region than in the rest of the area. This attracts more termites to that region, depositing more lumps of earth, and the positive feedback produced soon snowballs the process until one of the large termite pillars has come into being, all as a result of the initial fluctuation in the random scurrying.

This provides an example of how symmetry is broken by the effect of fluctuations.[22] Originally all points in the area occupied by the termites were on an equal, or symmetrical, footing. By chance one is selected as being special and becomes the site of the nest pillar, thereby breaking the original symmetry. Something similar happens in the cooling of heated ferromagnetic material. The material contains many small spinning systems which act as dipoles, that is, very tiny magnets. Each magnet on its own is free to point in any direction it likes. It is not restricted to a particular direction. (In this discussion we are neglecting the effects of the Earth's magnetic field.) At high temperatures the little magnets move freely and so their random orientations cancel each other out. This is the quenching of magnetism that results from heating. As the material cools, however, the magnets become less mobile. If a fluctuation causes a few to point in the same direction, their combined field then helps to align others and so over a whole domain the magnets approximately line up with each other. The individual magnet's lack of preference for any particular direction is overcome by this collaborative effect due to a fluctuation. Within the domain there is the preferred direction of its actual magnetization. Thus cooling restores the bulk magnetic property and breaks the perfect symmetry of the individual systems composing the bulk. Analogous symmetry breaking on a cosmic scale occurred when the Grand Unified Theory 'crystallized out' in the early history of the universe (p. 34). The process is called 'spontaneous symmetry breaking', because its details are not foreseeable but depend upon the precise character of the triggering fluctuation.

Subtle interweaving of chaos and order characterizes the whole range of these phenomena. In the magnetic material the individual dipoles have a perfect spherical symmetry (no preferred direction) but at high temperatures the enjoyment of this symmetry on the microscopic scale wipes out the possibility of the magnetism being manifested macroscopically. At lower temperatures chaos (a fluctuation) triggers order (domain magnetization) which destroys the symmetry but creates the long-range pattern (alignment of dipoles) which makes the material's magnetism macroscopically apparent.

Order can arise from chaos also simply by the effect of statistical regularities, that is from the fact that, for many systems with a large number of random elements in their composition, the most probable state is overwhelmingly most likely to occur and can be characterized by a certain overall pattern of a foreseeable form. A simple example of this occurring is provided by dropping a sequence of small balls from the same opening on to a vertical array of regularly spaced nails and allowing the balls to find their way to the bottom. Since the path depends very sensitively upon small details of the balls' direction of motion, each such path is essentially random. However the balls accumulate at the bottom in a pattern which quickly assumes the predictable bell-shaped curve that the statisticians call a Gaussian distribution. Although each individual event is unpredictable, the sum of many such events takes a form that can be forecast to a high degree of accuracy. Many acts of chaos add together to give a predictable order. The statistician Bartholomew is so impressed by this fact that he says, commenting about the order of the world, 'the point we wish to challenge is whether it *is* conceivable that the cosmos might have been a self-subsistent and determinate chaos . . . chaos and order are complementary; the presence of one seems to imply the other.[23] That may be so as far as macroscopic systems are concerned but when we spoke in the previous chapter about the marvellous rational intelligibility of the world, it was to microscopic order, such as the laws of elementary particle physics, that we were appealing. There seems no way to attribute these foundational patterns of regularity to statistical effects. They are intrinsic and call for some sort of reasonable explanation of a different kind from that afforded by probability theory.

The most striking example of all of the fruitful interrelation of randomness and orderliness is provided by the insight that it is the interplay of chance and necessity which characterizes the evolution of the universe (galaxies and stars are gravitationally enhanced fluctuations – cosmic termite nests, one might say) and of life (replicating molecules aggregating in the amino acid soup of early Earth) and of humanity (natural selection of genetic mutations). The significance to be attributed to these facts has been widely debated with conflicting conclusions.[24] To some, such as Jacques Monod, the role of chance is evidence of meaninglessness in the process of the world. To others of us it has seemed that the potentiality thereby exhibited as being inherent in the properties of matter – a potentiality which is explored through the shuffling operations of chance – is so remarkable as to constitute an insight of design present in the structure of the world. I have written elsewhere:

> When I read Monod's book I was greatly excited by the scientific picture it presented. Instead of seeing chance as an indication of the purposelessness and futility of the world, I was deeply moved by the thought of the astonishing fruitfulness it revealed inherent in the laws of atomic physics . . . the fact that they have such remarkable consequences as you and me speaks of the amazing potentiality contained in their structure. From this point of view the action of chance is to explore and realize that inherent fruitfulness.[25]

In the phrase 'chance and necessity' the word 'chance' does not signify a cause in itself but is used as a shorthand for a number of different processes. These include such occurrences as random quantum events, small fluctuations which trigger instabilities, the accidental impinging of independent causal chains (as would have happened to influence evolution if it is true, as some believe, that dinosaurs were wiped out by the collision of a large meteor with the Earth many millions of years ago) and, finally and most generally, just the way in which bits of matter interact with each other to produce a succession of configurations. Chance in this last sense is the occurrence of a sequence of uncorrelated possibilities. (The process is analogous to the way in which shuffling and dealing cards produces a succession of different hands at bridge.) The raw material of novelty thus provided by chance is then explored by the intervention of lawful necessity to sift and preserve those configurations which manifest their fruitfulness by their survival and replication in a regularly behaving environment. (This is like playing out the resulting bridge hands according to the rules of that game.) Thus the potentiality of the universe is brought to actuality, although the particular ways in which this happens depend on the accidental features of history, that is the particular details of the modes in which the triggers of chance have operated. (The potentiality of the game of bridge is discovered by playing it, though only a small proportion of all possible hands is ever encountered by any one player, so that there is an unpredictable element in his bridge experience.)

This chapter has portrayed a world whose processes can assemble complexity within a decaying environment and where random events can prove to be the originators of pattern. Such a world is a world of orderliness but not of clockwork regularity, of potentiality without predictability, endowed with an assurance of development but with a certain openness as to its actual form. It is inevitably a world with ragged edges, where order and disorder interlace each other and where the exploration of possibility by chance will lead not only to the evolution of systems of increasing complexity, endowed with new possibilities, but also to the evolution of systems imperfectly formed and malfunctioning. The former superior entities will earn the epithet 'successful' by their survival in the competition for constituent resources; the latter inferior entities will disappear from the evolving scene. It is just such a world that we live in.

The presence in it of physical evils (earthquakes, genetically induced malformations, disease) reflects the untidiness of disorder, just as the presence in it of physical goods (healthy conscious beings, a rich variety of plant and animal life) reflects the organizing power of order. Each is the inescapable complement of the other in the process of the world. 'However perplexing may be the existence of moral evil (the chosen cruelties of men) the problem of physical evil is solved by its being made intelligible as a by-product of the evolving interaction of chance and necessity.' So speak those who subscribe to a view that Cowburn[26] characterizes as 'evolutionary optimism'. Teilhard de Chardin saw things that way, so that he could write: 'In this new setting [that of evolutionary process], while evil loses nothing of its poignancy or horror, it ceases to be an incomprehensible element in the structure of the world and becomes a *natural feature*.'[27] Such a view is endorsed by Lonergan, who goes even further by asserting:

> But the proper criterion of the good is intelligibility and in the universe everything but basic sin [which is what we have called moral evil] can be understood and so is good. For the imperfection of the lower is the potentiality for the higher . . . So it is that a generalized emergent probability [Lonergan's phrase for the interactive process of chance and necessity] can be grasped even by our limited understanding as an immanently and highly intelligible order embracing everything in our universe.[28]

It would be difficult to put that to someone dying of a painful cancer. Lonergan's creed of *tout comprehendre c'est tout accepter* may satisfy the philosopher but will it really satisfy the theologian? What are we to make of the Creator of this strange world governed by both chance and necessity, being and becoming? The old image of the divine Clockmaker presiding over a steadily ticking universe has been replaced by One responsible for a world at once more open to innovation in its process and more dangerously precarious in its possible outcome. We must turn our attention to the theological implications of order and disorder, in the chapter that follows.

4

Creation and Creator

The preceding chapter surveyed the process of the world as it is discerned by science. Its unfolding is characterized by both order and disorder, subtly intertwined. Theology asserts that world to be a creation, so that its process is the expression of a Creator's purpose. Theology also proclaims that Creator to be good and almighty. Can such a claim be sustained in the face of the way things actually are?

In Christian theology the Creator is said to be free in the exercise of his will, so that there is no ineluctable constraint upon his act of creation. There is no world of Platonic forms imposing upon him an inescapably necessary order within which he must operate, nor is there independent brute manner (*hylē*) resisting and frustrating his purpose, as the Greeks had supposed. Everything in the world – its form and its substance, the nature of law and the nature of matter – is contingent upon his will alone.

The freedom thus asserted is the exterior freedom of God. He is not acted upon by any external agency in a way that limits his power or perturbs his will. He is neither thwarted by the opposition of an antigod (as dualism supposes) nor is he to be manipulated in his purpose (as magic claims). Yet the God who is eternally free is not an imperious dictator exercising an arbitrary will. He is *internally* constrained by the consistency of his own nature. His omnipotence is rightly understood as the ability to do what he wills, but he can only will what is in accord with his character. The rational God must respect reason. Descartes once went so far as to say: 'The mathematical verities are as much fixed by God, and depend as much on Him, as all the other creatures.'[1] Whatever that might mean it cannot imply that God is a logical despot, capable of decreeing that $2 + 2 = 5$. Most people would agree with that conclusion. It is also necessary to note that there are other self-consistent constraints upon God's action. The one who is faithful must show reliability in his relationship with his world. He will not be an arbitrary intervener in its processes but they will have about them a consistency which reflects his character. On this view the laws of nature are signs of God's fidelity.[2] The one who is love will grant a generous measure of independence to his world, for love is grounded in the free interchange between lover and beloved. The God of love can be no cosmic puppet master, pulling the strings of a world which is totally subservient to him.

It is clear that the balance between these internal constraints is a delicate one. Faithfulness might be expected to find its expression in order but a genuine freedom granted to the world opens up the possibility of disorder. It is important to recognize that God's love for the world in creation, though including humanity, is not exclusively man-centred. The universe is not just a gigantic theatre in which the human play is being performed after an overture lasting fifteen thousand million years. Therefore if these divine characteristics find their expression in creation it will be so cosmically as well as anthropologically. What this could possibly mean is something that we have to explore in this chapter. The world created by the God of love and faithfulness may be expected to be characterized both by the openness of chance and the regularity of necessity.

There is an obvious perplexity about what we have been saying so far. If God is constrained by the need to be rational, faithful, loving and so on, are we not making Reason, Fidelity, Love and the rest, rulers over him? Have we not restored the Platonic world of pre-existent forms as constraints upon divinity? Perhaps the answer lies simply in refusing to make the implied separation. Reason, Fidelity, Love cohere in God since he is the ground of all reality, but they are not mere tautologies for what he thinks, does and wills. We are already tangled in a web of anthropomorphism, as the last sentence all too clearly shows, and perhaps we need the Gordian-knot cutting scissors of apophatic theology, with its assertion of the unknowable otherness of God, to set us free. Of course our rational prattle is inadequate to discourse of the divine nature, but he is not so wholly Other that the declaration of his reason, faithfulness and love has no meaning for us. They point us in the right direction and yield a mutually interpretative fruitfulness in relation to our understanding of God's ways with his world.

A classical problem of theology is to inquire why God created a world at all. If he is self-consistent perfection, what need can he have of anything outside himself? This is a particular difficulty for Christian theology whose doctrine of the Holy Trinity speaks of an activity of love within the Godhead, in the mutual relationship of the Persons, needing no external augmentation. Yet the more one emphasizes the superfluity of the world in relation to the essential nature of God, the more its actual existence needs to be attributed to the generosity of love as its sole adequate ground, for what other reason could there be? The more complete God is seen to be in himself, the more his act of creation is perceived as an act of supererogation, only attributable to love.

An alternative answer was suggested by emanationism, the idea that the world was in some sense a kind of boiling-over of the divine at its periphery, a phenomenon on the fringe of deity, at its attentuated edge. What this might mean is not very clear. A closely related notion is that of panentheism (the idea that the world is part of God but not the whole of God), which exerts a substantial influence on contemporary theology.[3] Its attraction is that it overcomes theology's perpetual temptation to distance God from the world in splendid but isolated perfection. Panentheism places emphasis on the imperative of love to seek response. Moltmann says of the 'creative love, which communicates itself by overcoming its opposite, which "gives life to the dead and calls into existence the things that do not exist" (Rom. 4,17)':

Is not this the reason why the divine love presses even beyond the Trinity? Does it not seek its 'image', which is to say its response and therefore its bliss, in men and women?[4]

(Note the anthropocentricity of this view of God's creative activity.) But he goes on to criticize panentheism because:

The process of the world is then identified with the inner Trinitarian life of God, and vice versa; the world process is the eternal life of God himself . . . The elements of truth in this view are turned into their opposite once the capacity to distinguish is suppressed by the will to synthesis.[5]

Panentheism's defect is its denial of the true otherness of the world from God, which is part of our experience. The classical doctrine of creation, with its assertion of the world's freedom to be itself over against God, but yet of its contingent dependence upon him for its existence, is surely the better understanding. As we continue to explore its possible meaning we shall find that it will be able to do justice in a remarkable way to the need we feel to involve God intimately with the fate of his world, to make that world not only, as Calvin said, 'the theatre of his glory', but also the theatre of his love.

The act of creation is a continuing process. We reject the deistic idea that God simply lit the blue touch paper to set off the big bang and then left the world to its own devices. Such an idea attributes too great a degree of autonomy to the world and to the laws which govern its process. The Christian understanding is that the cosmos is not self-sustaining but is kept in being by a continuous act of will by its Creator. Too great a concentration on the first two chapters of Genesis, or an inadequate interpretation of them, has sometimes misled Christians into placing undue emphasis on a doctrine of creation conceived of as a doctrine of temporal origin. Hence the erroneous thought that big bang cosmology, with its dateable point of departure for the universe as we know it, has a superior value for theology over the steady-state theory, which essentially supposed the universe to have been everlasting. The latter has now been discredited since the discovery in 1965 of the background cosmic radiation, a sort of re-echoing whisper of that far-off explosive era of the big bang. Yet theology could have lived with either physical theory, for the assertion that God is Creator is not a statement that at a particular time he did something, but rather that at all times he keeps the world in being. The doctrine of creation is a doctrine of ontological origin. Just as we have learnt to understand Genesis 3 as a statement of man's ever-contemporary experience of alienation from the ground of being, rather than an aetiological explanation of that experience as the consequence of a catastrophic past event, so we must understand from Genesis 1 and 2 that the world and its process are a continual expression of the creative will of God. Such a view finds more explicit expression in other parts of the Bible, particularly in the psalms. Psalm 104, speaking of all living creatures, says:

When thou hidest thy face, they are dismayed;
when thou takest away their breath, they die and return to their dust.
When thou sendest forth thy spirit, they are created;
and thou renewest the face of the ground.[6]

It is a moving expression of dependence on God. In the much wider cosmic history that we are able to survey, the actualization of the potentiality with which matter is endowed, exhibited by the coming-to-be of complex organization through the evolving process of the world, is a sign of God's unendingly spoken creative word 'Let there be . . .' A 'celebrated author and divine' who had struggled within the framework of his Christian faith to come to terms with the insights of evolutionary biology, wrote to Charles Darwin:

> I have gradually learnt to see that it is as noble a conception of the Deity to believe that He created a few original forms capable of self-development into other and needful forms, as to believe that He required a fresh act of creation to supply the voids caused by the actions of His laws.[7]

He was thinking of elementary germs of life. We can now extend his thought to encompass as our primal forms the quarks and gluons and electrons which are the very constituents of matter. All that marvellous tale, from big bang to *homo sapiens* and on to whatever lies in the future, is the story of creation. Macquarrie writes that 'as philosophers from Plotinus to Whitehead have pointed out, inert formless matter cannot evolve into a universe as we know it'.[8] But the matter revealed to the inquiry of modern science is neither inert nor formless. Its pattern-creating dance is in accordance with laws capable of astonishing fruitfulness in their consequences, laws which we have already claimed to be pale reflections of the faithfulness of the Creator who moment by moment ordains that they should be so.

The God conceived of in these terms as Creator is as far as possible from any idea of a demiurge. The latter is a cause among causes, an agent among the many agencies at work in the world, even if he possesses power and intelligence greatly superior to the other actors on the cosmic stage. The Creator God, on the other hand, is the author and producer of the whole play.

The demiurge, the intelligent contriver and manipulator of material resources which are there at his disposal but not at his command, is a surprisingly popular figure in modern thought about the process of the world. Paul Davies writes:

> Those who invoke God as an explanation of cosmic organization usually have in mind a *super-natural* agency, acting on the world in de-

fiance of natural laws. But it is perfectly possible for much, if not all, of what we encounter in the universe to be the product of intelligent manipulation of a purely natural kind: within the laws of physics.[9]

It will be clear that Davies's supernatural God, the celestial conjurer working against the grain of natural law, bears no relation to the Christian God who is the ground of natural law. It is his second possibility, the 'natural God' as he calls it, which represents the appeal to a demiurge. Concerning him Davies says:

> He would not be omnipotent for he could not act outside the laws of nature. He would be the creator of everything we see, having made matter from pre-existing energy, organized it appropriately, set up the conditions necessary for life to develop and so on, but he would not be capable of creation out of nothing (*ex nihilo*) as the Christian doctrine requires.[10]

Davies's demiurge would possess some pretty remarkable powers but he points out one limitation that such a 'God' would be subject to. He would not be able to prevent the eventual decay of the universe (a topic we shall return to later). In a highly curious book, Fred Hoyle thinks along somewhat similar lines. He writes: '"God" is a forbidden word in science, but if we define an intelligence superior to ourselves as deity, then in this book we have arrived at two kinds.'[11] Those two 'Gods' are a contriver similar to Davies's natural God, and a mysterious teleological influence acting from the future to draw the universe towards its eventual fulfilment. To our surprise, Hoyle joins Teilhard de Chardin in peering forward to the omega point.[12] I suspect that one reason why these scientists incline to the fanciful idea of a demiurgic intelligence at work is that they (most unscientifically) are unwilling to take account of the evidence of religious experience which would point them to the knowledge of a God transcendentally other and yet the ground of cosmic process.

Another popular way of thinking about a demiurge is to picture him at work in the world as the arranger of fruitful coincidence. A posited influence such as Jung's synchronicity,[13] the acausal origin of events otherwise attributed to pure chance, is playing just such a role. The God of Whitehead's thought is not free from similar limited characterization. Commenting on this, Macquarrie writes: 'Whitehead's

God is not ultimate – he is one actual entity among many, admittedly unique, yet coordinate with the world, so that "it is as true to say that God creates the world as that the world creates God".[14] Christian writers wishing to emphasize the role of the Holy Spirit, the immanent presence of God in the world, have sometimes fallen into a similar manner of speaking. Hugh Montefiore wrote:

> Although there is no external force imposed on species, and in particular on their genetic systems, mutations occur which would not be expected by random mutation. This is not because of external pressures but because of the bias implanted in matter. Such a bias is not, of course, to be detected by scientific measurement (and so the hypothesis is not testable) since there is no possibility of setting it alongside matter which is not implanted with this bias towards complexity and organization. Another way of describing this bias would be to call it the Holy Spirit working within the matter of the universe, unfolding the purpose of the Creator by immanent operation.[15]

But if there is such a 'bias' it is revealed by comparison with the calculated odds of random events. Its presence surely then suggests the presence of effects not correctly taken into account in calculating those probabilities. (The die keeps on falling with the 6 face upwards . . . but the die is loaded.) The question of whether such effects are present is a scientifically posable question and I see no reason why it should not be expected to receive a scientifically stateable answer. There may well be more to evolution than has met the neo-Darwinian eye, but to call that missing ingredient in our understanding the Holy Spirit is to invoke the God of the Gaps.

If there are demiurgic intelligences at work in the universe they are agents among other agencies and their nature and mode of operation should, in principle, be as open to scientific inquiry as that of any other participant in the process of the world. Most of those who invoke the notion are extremely uninformative about how their particular demiurge might achieve his purpose. Even the scientists are pretty vague. Davies says:

> The origin of galaxies, for example, has no satisfactory explanation at present. The origin of life is another baffling puzzle. But we can

conceive of both these systems being deliberately engineered by an intelligent superbeing, without any violation of the laws of physics.[16]

The language is as anthropomorphic as saying 'the Lord God formed man of dust from the ground'.[17] The nature and action of this superbeing is left totally without explanation. Hoyle considers that one of his 'gods' (the teleological one in the future) might operate by being the cause of 'uncaused' quantum events,[18] an idea of a sort of divine psychokinesis at the cloudy constituent roots of the universe which William Pollard also tried to adopt for explaining the action of the Christian God upon his world.[19] The idea of such a hole-and-corner deity, fiddling around at the rickety roots of the cosmos, has not commended itself to many.[20]

One way of expressing the character of the Creator is to speak of him as the one who lets be, or as Being itself. Macquarrie describes the idea thus: 'Being is not something that is but rather the letting-be that is prior to any is-ness'.[21] Exactly what this means is not altogether clear. Perhaps an analogy drawn from physics might be helpful. Our modern understanding of the nature of matter is framed in terms of quantum field theory. A field is an entity taking values at every point of space and instant of time, a truly extended physical system. In a quantum field (that is, one whose dynamical behaviour is described by quantum mechanics) the excitations of the field (that is, the 'blips' of energy present in the field) take a particular form that enables them to be interpreted as particles, countable packets of energy. Thus quantum field theory successfully synthesizes wave (field) and particle (blip).[22] The field itself is characterized by certain mathematical equations which determine the nature of the particles present in that particular field. We could think of the field as the letting-be that enables the is-ness of its particle excitations to occur. You may find that notion too far from your own thought to be helpful, but for me it affords some analogical clue to what talk of Being might amount to. To take it more seriously than that would be to regard quantum fields as the 'sensorium of God' (in the way that Newton was emboldened to talk about absolute space), a panentheistic idea which does not commend itself to me. When all is said and done, quantum fields are simply creatures.

Such a reminder is relevant to a certain amount of scientific talk which has been going on and which claims to impinge on another theological mode of expression which asserts the otherness of the world in relation to God. That is the claim that God created the universe *ex nihilo*, out of nothing. The material world sprang into being, and is maintained in being, by his command alone. With its emergence came spacetime itself, for it is linked with matter in a way that was articulated scientifically by Einstein in his General Theory of Relativity. Augustine had realized that this would have to be so some fifteen hundred years previously. He wrote, 'There is no time before the world began', just as 'There is no space beyond this world', because 'without motion and change there is no time'.[23]

Ingenious theoretical physicists have proposed a scheme for the world's emergence from 'nothing' as a quantum fluctuation.[24] With characteristic lack of solemnity Alan Guth has referred to such ideas as the universe's turning out to be a 'free lunch'. The idea is to exploit the strange properties of the vacuum in quantum theory. It is not true in that theory that if there is nothing there then nothing is happening. Quite the contrary, for the quantum vacuum is a hive of activity, full of fluctuations, random comings-to-be and fadings-away. It is easier to indicate how this comes about by considering a very elementary physical system, the simple pendulum. Its 'vacuum' (that is to say, its lowest energy state) would, according to Newton, be just that in which the bob is at rest and at the bottom. For a quantum pendulum, Heisenberg does not permit that, for we would then both know where the bob is (at the bottom) and what it is doing (it is at rest). Such detailed knowledge would contradict the uncertainty principle. Consequently the lowest energy state of a quantum pendulum is one in which there is a fuzzy vibration – almost at the bottom and nearly at rest, but not quite. Augmented to the complexity of quantum field theory, this fuzzy vibration produces the fluctuating vacuum of which I have spoken. There are no particles present, no permanent excitations, but there is a continual chaos of transient blips, rising and falling away again. If one of these excitations were particularly big, it might get blown up by the effects of inflation (p. 23) to cosmic proportions! On this view we would be living in a grotesquely swollen quantum fluctuation.

Needless to say the notion is speculative to the highest degree, a wild idea with many difficulties and no certainty whatever of proving correct. However, suppose for a moment that such a fluctuation was the actual origin of our universe. It would certainly not have come from something which without great abuse of language could be called 'nothing'. There has to be a quantum field (or actually, because of the complexity of our world, many quantum fields) given as the source of the fluctuation. The price of the 'free lunch' is the provision of those quantum fields. On a Christian understanding that provision would be the continuing act of the Creator.

Quantum fields are highly structured entities. The voice of unbridled speculation goes on to inquire whether it might not be that they have emerged from some chance combination of pre-cosmic 'bits', random concatenations of discrete 'events' which fortuitously order themselves into a coherent pattern. To talk thus is to carry speculation to the point of incoherence and beyond. One cannot call such thinking scientific, though some scientists have indulged in it.[25] So have the process theologians:

> Process theology rejects the notion of *creatio ex nihilo*, if that means creation out of *absolute* nothingness . . . Process theology affirms instead a doctrine of creation out of chaos. . . A state of absolute chaos would be one in which nothing but very lowgrade actual occasions happening at random, i.e. without being ordered into enduring individuals.[26]

The ghost of the Greek *hylē* lingers on. The Creator is again reduced to a contriving demiurge. Such a view seems to me to be just an unconvincing resistance to allowing God to be God. The starting-point for our discussion of the cosmos can either be God or structured matter (depending on the depth of understanding we are seeking); a shadowy domain between the two totally lacks motivation from our actual knowledge and experience of the world.

One of the main concerns of process theology is to find a place for the temporal and contingent within God. This is an essential task for any theology which recognizes that a solely necessary being could never be the source of contingent creation, since all his acts would themselves be necessary. Keith Ward says, 'The truly contingent cannot arise from the wholly necessary . . . If God is the Creator of a contingent world, he must be contingent and temporal.' Process theology seeks to meet this demand by its idea of the consequent nature of God, evolving with the world. But that is only half the story. As Ward goes on to say, 'The demands of intelligibility [of the world] require the existence of a necessary, immutable, eternal being'[27] whose self-sustained rational reliability is the ground of the world's existence. This requirement is not fully met by the process theologians. They speak of God's primordial nature, but it is little more than a portfolio of potentialities. Ward says of Whitehead's God that he

> does not truly interact with the world; he includes it and provides the source of its possible futures and the reservoir of its completed experiences . . . the cosmic tyrant, against whom Whitehead so strongly protests, has become the cosmic sponge, absorbing all experiences but contributing nothing except an abstract array of external possibilities for the creative multiplicity of the world.[28]

Ward's book, *Rational Theology and the Creativity of God*, from which these quotations are drawn, is a sustained, and in my view very helpful, attempt to articulate the idea of a God whose internal complexity is such that he can embrace both the necessary and the contingent, the eternal and the temporal. Such an understanding has the result that 'Once one accepts the idea of a temporal, everlasting God, one is committed to explaining the finite world, partly as governed in its existence and structure by his necessary nature, and partly expressing his freely chosen purpose.'[29] This divine complementarity of being and becoming is the theological counterpart of the chance and necessity that the scientist discerns in the process of the world.

In the act of creation God makes room for something other than himself. Naturally, we are speaking of an ontological making way, not a spatial shrinkage. Moltmann says that 'It is only God's withdrawal into himself which gives that *nihil* the space in which God becomes creatively active'. Yet that withdrawal is not an act of abandonment. Quite the reverse, for

> Must we not say that this 'Creation outside God' exists simultaneously *in God*, in the space which God has made for it in his omnipresence? Has God not therefore created the world 'in himself', giving it time *in* his eternity, finitude *in* his infinity, space *in* his omnipresence and freedom *in* his selfless love?[30]

Thus Moltmann attempts the difficult but essential task of trying to preserve both the independence of creation and its Creator's intimate involvement with it. He goes on to refer to the thought of the Jewish Kabbalist, Isaac Luria, whose doctrine of *zimsum* (concentration or contraction) led him to say that 'the existence of the universe was made possible by a shrinkage process in God'.

We encounter here an idea of the greatest importance, the understanding that the act of creation involves a *kenosis* of God, an emptying of himself and an acceptance of the self-limitation inherent in the giving of creative love. This insight finds striking, even excessive, expression in the writings of W. H. Vanstone.

> Nothing [he writes] must be withheld from the self-giving which is creation: no unexpended reserves of divine power or potentiality: no 'glory of God' or 'majesty of God' which may be compared and contrasted with the glory of the galaxies or the majesty of the universe; no 'power of God' which might exceed and over-ride the God-given power of the universe: no 'eternity of God' which might outlive an eternal universe.[31]

These are hard words in their uncompromising assertion of the risk involved in creation. Vanstone quotes the line of the *Dies Irae*: *Tantus labor non sit cassus* (May so great a labour not be in vain) and applies it, not to the saving passion of Christ as in the original, but to the Father's act of calling the world to be. There is a vulnerability involved in creation which God freely embraces:

> The activity of God in creation must be precarious. It must proceed by no assured programme. Its progress, like every progress of love, must be an angular progress – in which each step is a precarious step into the unknown . . . If the creation is the work of love, then its shape cannot be predetermined by the Creator, nor its triumph foreknown: it is the realization of vision, but of vision which is discovered only through its own realization: all faith in its triumph is neither more or less than faith in the Creator Himself – faith that He will not cease from His handiwork nor abandon the object of His love.[32]

Vanstone makes no reference to the modern understanding of the interplay of order and disorder, chance and necessity, in the process of the world. Yet the picture that physical insight presents of a universe exploring its inherent potentiality through the shuffling operations of chance, proving fruitful in its outcome in ways not foreseeable in advance, is strikingly consonant with the concept of creation as 'the realization of vision, but of vision which is discovered only through its own realization'. Commenting on the role of chance in cosmic evolution, Bartholomew says it made it necessary 'to formulate a doctrine of providence which, allowing that God is ultimately responsible for everything that happens, did not require his intimate involvement in all things.'[33] To put the matter in terms of human concern, God has created a world in which cancer can occur but he is not the agent through which it strikes the individual. Its incidence is not his determinate act but he is responsible for allowing the world to be such that it can happen. The answer to Job is not the Jungian antinomy of good and evil within God,[34] but the antinomy of chance and necessity within the freely evolving creation that he allows to be.

In other words, God chose a world in which chance has a role to play, thereby both being responsible for the consequences accruing and also accepting limitation of his power to control. Pannenberg speaks of just such a God who is made known in the person and history of Jesus Christ. In contrast to the God of the philosophers: 'He is revealed, not as the unchangeable ultimate ground of the phenomenal order, but as the free origin of the contingent events of the world, whose interrelations are contingent and constitute no eternal order but a history moving forward from event to event.'[35] I would want to say that he is revealed in *both* those modes, as 'ground of the phenomenal order' and as 'free origin of contingent events', the God of necessity and the God of chance, the ground of both being and becoming, the One who is at once reliable and vulnerable. Though God was under no compulsion to undertake the risk of creation, by that free act the world has become necessary to him and he is intimately involved with its fate. Vanstone compares this to the way in which the act of adoption makes a child necessary to a family, and his welfare the active object of their concern, whilst before that deed of adoption the family was complete in itself.

The interplay of chance and necessity as the means by which the free process of the world realizes itself has already been seen as offering some degree of understanding of the presence of physical evils in the world (p. 49). Vanstone acknowledges this when he writes: 'The existence of evil must be seen as the expression or consequence of the precariousness of the divine creativity. Evil is the moment of control jeopardized and lost; and the redemption of evil is inseparable from the process of creation.'[36] To speak thus is not to attribute the ills of the world to the recalcitrance of matter (the brute resistance of *hylē*) in opposition to the divine will, but to recognize, as in the case of human artistic creativity, that the choice of medium imposes its own constraint. Men and women are the most outstanding examples known to us of the power of matter -in-organization to bring about conceptual novelty. Out of the raw material of quarks and gluons and electrons have come beings transcending their origin by the capacity for self-consciousness and enabled both to know the nature of the matter of which they are made and to worship the Creator who endowed it with such marvellous potentiality. That is surely the coming-to-be of a great good. We have no reason to suppose – given that by his nature God is a God of process and not of magic – that good to have been capable of achievement without the long cosmic history of the interplay of chance and necessity, with all its prodigality and blind alleys, which produced both humankind and the perilous environment in which it lives.

The God of process is to be thought of as the one who is achieving his purpose through the evolution of the world that he maintains in being. This places considerable emphasis on teleology, the eventual accomplishment of the *telos*, the perfect fulfilment. Pannenberg writes, 'According to the Biblical understanding, the essence of things will be decided only in the future. What they are is decided by what they will become. Thus creation happens from the end, from the ultimate future.'[37] It would be disingenuous not to point out that our scientific understanding of the eventual fate of the universe puts in question any facile understanding of those words in terms of an unfolding of the present world process. The cosmic future looks pretty bleak. The history of the universe, from the moment of the big bang onwards, has been a tug-of-war between two opposing tendencies. One is the expansive force of the big bang itself, throwing matter apart. The other is the force of gravity, pulling matter together. They are closely balanced and we are not sure which will win in the end. If expansion gains a marginal victory, then the galaxies will continue to fly apart for ever. Within themselves they will condense into gigantic black holes. Through the possible decay of nuclear matter, and through the expected decay of black holes via Hawking radiation, the world will, after an immense period of time, simply run down and end up in the modern version of its heat death. On the other hand, if the forces of attraction gain a marginal victory, then the present expansion of the universe will eventually be halted and reversed. After many thousands of millions of years, what started with the big bang will end in the big crunch as the world collapses in upon itself. Either way the prospects are bleak. If the 'essence of things will be decided only in the future' then that essence, as we perceive it within the scenario of the present world, is found to be one of futility. On a cosmic scale the Preacher was right: 'Vanity of vanities! All is vanity'.[38]

What we are to make of this gloomy prognosis for the future of the universe? It is the cosmic counterpart of the human certainty that as individuals we shall all surely die. Christian hope is not denied by the recognition of the impending dissolution of our bodies. For those of us who believe in the resurrection of the body there is the hope of a destiny beyond death in which the information-bearing pattern (which is the persisting element of ourselves continuing through the ceaseless changes in the matter making up our bodies) will be recreated in an unimaginable new environment of God's choosing. The eventual decay of the universe simply reminds us that it is as true cosmically as it is anthropologically that 'if for this life only we have hope in Christ, we are of all men most to be pitied'.[39] One of the themes of this book is that God's purpose in creation must be construed, not narrowly in terms of humankind alone, but in the widest possible terms embracing the whole universe. That must also be true of the redemption which brings about the *telos*, the true fulfilment of the whole process. The creation of the physical world is not a merely transient episode but matter must have its destiny too, along with men. What this means is clearly beyond our powers to anticipate. St Paul seems to be striving after such an idea when he wrote these mysterious words to the Romans:

> The creation waits with eager longing for the revealing of the sons of God; for the creation was subjected to futility, not of its own will but by the will of him who subjected it in hope; because the creation itself will be set free from its bondage to decay and obtain the glorious liberty of the children of God.[40]

What Paul Davies's natural God is unable to do, the true and living God will accomplish.

But if all will find fulfilment in the New Creation, why do we have first to endure the imperfections of the old? An answer might lie, as I have written elsewhere, 'in the patience of a God content to achieve his purposes through the unfolding of process. It is possible that Love can only work in such a way, out of respect for the beloved.'[41] We are called by God to share with him in the vulnerability of his act of creation because only by such acceptance can the One who acts by the lure of love rather than by the force of magic accomplish in us and in his whole world his purpose of good. The only life which is free from error and frustration is the perfect life of the omniscient and omnipotent God. The Orthodox theologians tell us that the true end of creation lies in deification. The precarious path we travel is the cosmic Pilgrim's Progress whence that for which God 'made room' finds its way back to him, to find its fulfilment, not in absorption, but in a freely embraced union which could be entered into in no other way.

It is time to try to sum things up. The opening chapters of three of the books of the New Testament present Jesus Christ as the agent both of creation and of salvation. They are the prologue to John (John 1.1–18), the christological hymn of Colossians (Col. 1.15–20) and the opening verses of the Epistle to the Hebrews (Heb. 1.1–5). John speaks of the divine Word through whom all things were made and who was made flesh in the man Jesus of Nazareth. Paul[42] speaks of the cosmic Christ who is before all things and in whom all things hold together. The writer to the Hebrews speaks of the Son who upholds the universe by the word of his power. There is a strong element of Old Testament wisdom thought lying behind all three passages. What gives them their unique Christian significance is the assertion that the divine Principle thus spoken about has been manifested in human terms as Jesus Christ. This has important implications for what we have been discussing, for the incarnation testifies to God's deepest possible involvement with his creation. I believe that the empty tomb – which speaks to us of the Lord's risen body being formed by the transmutation and glorification of his dead body – holds forth the hope of a destiny for matter as well as for men. The great symbol of the ascension is a vision of humanity (and so, temporality) being caught up into God. Torrance says that 'In the risen Christ . . . there is involved a hypostatic union between eternity and time'.[43] In these ways Scripture speaks to our present concerns.

The full interpretation of these passages will require not only consideration of their philosophical and theological background but also the scientific inspection of the world thus asserted to be upheld by Christ. Pannenberg has criticized any attempt to revive a *Logos* Christology by saying:

> The laws of contemporary physics are inherent in the processes they describe; they do not transcend them and are hardly mediators of divinity! . . . If one worked to produce an analogy with the patristic Logos Christology, namely in connection with the thought of contemporary natural science, one would have to begin by understanding the laws of nature, contrary to the self-understanding of natural science, as prototypes existing beyond and not fully expressed in the natural processes.[44]

I would reply to that by saying that the intelligible and delicately balanced structure of the world does raise questions which transcend the purely scientific and to this extent the laws of contemporary physics can, in their modest way, prove 'mediators of divinity'. They provoke an intellectual restlessness which will only find its quiet in a deeper rationality than that provided by natural science. The search for understanding is the search for the *Logos*. Swinburne says that 'for the theist explanation stops at what intuitively is the most natural stopping place for explanation – the choice of an agent'.[45]

Yet the order and disorder which intertwine in the process of the world show that the universe upheld by the divine Word is not a clear cold cosmos whose history is the inevitable unfolding of an invulnerable plan. It is a world kept in being by the divine Juggler rather than by the divine Structural Engineer, a world whose precarious process speaks of the free gift of Love. We are accustomed to think of the vulnerability accepted by the Word in the incarnation, a vulnerability potentially present in the baby lying in the manger and realized to the full in the man hanging on the cross. What is there revealed of the divine in the human life of Jesus is also to be discerned in the cosmic story of creation.

Paul tells us that it is God's purpose in Christ 'to reconcile to himself all things, whether in earth or in heaven'.[46] Talk of the cosmic Christ is not hyperbolic rhetoric but it points to the hope of redemption for the whole world process. Inspection of that world coheres with deep Christian insight. God's steadfast love is revealed in the synergy of chance and necessity. The potentiality of matter, by which fluctuations prove the triggers for the generation of order, indicates his purpose at work bringing about fulfilment amid the world's precarious process. The doctrine of creation so understood delivers us from a merely man-centred view of theology. Westermann wrote that 'once theology has imperceptibly become detached from Creator-Creation, the necessary consequence is that it must become an anthropology and begin to disintegrate from within, and collapse around us.'[47] The interaction of science and theology in constructing a doctrine of creation can save us from that dismal fate.

5

The Nature of Reality

In Chapter 2 I sought to characterize theological investigation as the search for understanding at the deepest possible level. Such a claim implies a whole-hearted acceptance of the unity of knowledge. In turn that requires the attainment of an harmonious and integrated view of the nature of reality. To put it in simple and directly personal terms, my experience as a physicist and my experience as a priest have to be capable of being held together, without compartmentalism or dishonest adjustment. I am not content just to say that in my scientific life I am concerned with the material universe, whilst in my ministry in the Church it is spiritual values which are the objects of my concern – and never mind how they relate to one another. 'No one can serve two masters.'[1] One's instinct to seek a unified view of reality is theologically underwritten by belief in the Creator who is the single ground of all that is. The rich complexity of creation demands an account of the world which will not deny proper respect to the nature of either the mental or the material. It must accommodate within its metaphysical embrace both the constituent insights of elementary particle physics and also the integrating insights of aesthetic and religious experience. It must do justice to human embedding in time, and to man's worshipful intuitions of eternity. Only by attempting to locate thought within such a comprehensive framework can we feel comfortable in considering those particular points of interaction between science and theology which have been our principal concern so far. At the very least we must have a tentative view of reality which holds together in a single account the varied subjects of our discourse.

To state the goal of our inquiry is by no means to imply that it will easily be attained. In fact, of course, if I were able to set before you such a universal understanding I would have achieved for myself an imperishable place in the history of thought. The actuality is rather different. The proportion of perplexity to insight in this chapter will be considerable, but for all that I do not feel unduly apologetic. The practice of science encourages one to think that it is better to hold together various puzzling pieces of experience, with respect for their stubborn facticity, and then make whatever shift one can to reconcile them, rather than to produce a tidy scheme by wilful oversimplification and neglect of evidence. The early investigators of quantum phenomena had to hang on by the skin of their intellectual teeth until eventually they found the harmonious resolution of threatened paradox.[2]

The nineteeth-century physicist contemplated a dual world of particles and waves. Newton told him how particles behaved; Maxwell laid down the equations governing the wave-like behaviour of the electromagnetic field. Both sorts of entity were necessary since Young's diffraction experiments had disproved the suggestion, somewhat cautiously advanced by Newton, that light might be made up of tiny particles. The discoveries of Planck and Einstein set in train a line of research which revealed that these apparently distinct possibilities interpenetrated each other. Light ejected electrons from metals in a way which could only be made sense of by adopting Einstein's interpretation that it was behaving like a beam of particles, each endowed with Planck's quantum of energy. Electrons did what de Broglie had suggested that they might do and were diffracted by a thin metal foil in a wave-like way. Eventually an understanding was achieved which saw wave and particle as complementary aspects of a single reality. Treat a quantum entity as a wave and it will oblige you with the appropriate behaviour; treat it like a particle and that will be the way in which it will be found to respond. Such seemingly fickle behaviour is nevertheless logically consistent because interrogation in the wave mode and interrogation in the particle mode are mutually exclusive experimental possibilities. You can employ one or the other but not both at once, so that contradiction is never encountered. Complementarity, as the quantum physicists call this delicate behaviour, is the scientist's equivalent of the theologian's *perichorēsis*, the mutual indwelling of characteristics.

Lifting our eyes from the particulars of physical science to the generalities of human experience, we contemplate a world which also seems to enjoy a dual character. We are aware of both mental phenomena and material phenomena. Of course our direct experience is always mental in character. Material bodies are constructs arising from our mentally organized apprehension of sense data. Yet so marvellously patterned is that experience that I for one cannot doubt that it is the discernment of an actual reality. I refuse to join the idealists in assigning an ontological priority to the mental over the material. I have written elsewhere, in defence of a critically realist view of science:

> The natural convincing explanation of the success of science is that it is gaining a tightening grasp of an actual reality. The true goal of scientific endeavour is understanding the structure of the physical world, an understanding which is never complete but ever capable of further improvement. The terms of that understanding are dictated by the way things are.[3]

There *is* a material world we can learn about.

Equally I refuse to join the physical reductionists in assigning reality only to the material and relegating the mental to a trivial epiphenomenal role:

> The reductionist programme in the end subverts itself. Ultimately it is suicidal . . . Thought is replaced by electro-chemical neural events. Two such events cannot confront each other in rational discourse. They are neither right nor wrong. They simply happen.[4]

The mental and the material are both to be given their due, but that desirable end will not be achieved satisfactorily by espousing a Cartesian dualism, simply setting them side by side and invoking the pineal gland, or divinely arranged synchronization, to explain the manifest correspondences between them. The act of the willed lifting of a hammer and its consequent use to render someone unconscious by a smart tap on the head make the existence of such correspondences only too clear. Cartesianism simply fails to explain how they come about in any way that carries conviction. Its twin worlds of extension and thought, matter and mind, fail to coalesce into the one world of our psychosomatic experience.

If it is neither mind nor matter nor mind-and-matter, what remains? The only possibility appears to be a complementary world of mind/matter in which these polar opposites cohere as contrasting aspects of the world-stuff, encountered in greater or lesser states of organization. If you take me apart you will find that all you get will be matter – in all the elusive subtlety that quantum mechanics has taught us to attribute to the material – matter ultimately found to be constituted of the quarks, gluons and electrons which compose all the rest of the physical universe. Neither soul nor entelechy will be found as a separate part of the residue. Yet if you want to encounter *me* you will have to refrain from that act of decomposition and accept me in my complex and delicately organized totality. That almost infinitely complex information-carrying pattern, which persists through all the changes of material constituents as nutrition and wear-and-tear ceaselessly replace the individual atoms of my body, and which by its very persistence expresses the true continuity of my person, that pattern is the meaning of the soul. It seems to me that this understanding corresponds closely to the Aristotelian notion of the soul as the 'form' of the body. St Thomas Aquinas felt that, while this would do very well for understanding the nature of animals, more was needed to do justice to humanity. 'Man', he wrote 'is non-material in respect of his intellectual power because the power of understanding is not the power of an organ.'[5] I do not see why that should be so. Understanding, self-consciousness, and the ability to know and worship the Creator may all be powers of that wonderfully subtle organ, the brain – or, better still, of the whole body – in striking illustration of the fertility of matter-in-organization. Such a view would accord well with the Hebrew understanding of the psychosomatic unity of man. It would also accord with the Christian hope of resurrection, the reconstruction of that pattern, dissolved by death, in a new environment of God's choosing.

The idea of complementarity in quantum theory was first clearly articulated by Neils Bohr. He went on in later life to advocate its application in wider contexts:

> In the account of psychical phenomena, we meet conditions of observation and corresponding means of expression still further removed from the terminology of physics . . . the word consciousness, applied to oneself as well as to others, is indispensable when describing the human condition. While the terminology adapted to orientation in the environment could take as its starting-point simple physical pictures and ideas of causality, the account of our states of mind required a typical complementary mode of description.[6]

Having said that, Bohr has nothing more to say.

There is a striking dissimilarity between Bohr on atomic physics and Bohr on human knowledge. In respect of physics he can explain perfectly how the complementary modes of description are related to each other, by means of the formalism of quantum theory and through the mutually incompatible arrangements of experimental inquiry that would be involved in their investigation. We know what is going on. In respect of human knowledge, complementarity is scarcely more than a slogan, an exhortation to look in a particular direction but not a specification of what we shall actually see if we do so. I have adopted that slogan and am peering in that direction. One catches an occasional glimpse of insight through the obscuring mists of ignorance.

Those who take the unified view of a material/mental world that I am advocating have sometimes felt driven to some form of panpsychism, the endowment of elementary matter with a residual prehensive power which in aggregation will lead to consciousness. David Griffin writes that: 'The difference between the proton and the psyche is one of degree, not of kind (in an ontological sense). One who holds otherwise is a dualist, however odious such a description may be.'[7] Griffin is a process theologian and the thought of A. N. Whitehead does indeed seem to have a panpsychic character. Events are basic to his metaphysics and each event is held to have a quasi-subjective phase (prehension) followed by an objectification (concrescence), a sort of wedding of the material and mental in the marriage-bed of occurrence. This seems to me to be an unhappily literal way of seeking a synthesis. It is not the case in quantum theory that every particle has a little bit of undulation in it, which when added together gives a wave. The mixture is more subtle. The number operator (which counts the particles) and the phase operator (which specifies the wave) are what are called conjugate variables. They do not commute and so are incapable of simultaneous quantifiability.[8] A wave-like state is, therefore, one with an *indefinite* number of particles in it.

That insight cannot be applied by direct analogy to the case we are considering. The mental is certainly not characterized by association with an indefinite quantity of the material. If there is any connection whatever between the ideas of quantum physics and those of a complementary metaphysics, it might rather lie in the mental being associated with an indefinite degree of organization of the material, a sort of openness of pattern. The participation of highly organized matter in the experience of the mental would result not merely from enhanced complexity of association but also from increased flexibility within that association. Some degree of support for this idea might be held to arise from the considerations of Chapter 3. There we were concerned with questions of becoming and the nature of time. Griffin says that 'The status of freedom, causality and time are in the same boat'[9] and it seems to me to be a sound intuition that there is an interrelationship of all these matters with our wider mental experience. In Prigogine's understanding of the nature of becoming an essential role is played by the presence of a degree of randomness in the system, due to the existence of multiple instabilities (p. 41). It is the consequent indefiniteness which brings about an openness to the future and a genuine novelty in the unfolding process of time. The great augmentation of potentiality in moving from simple thermodynamic systems to complex living beings might enable an enhanced openness of pattern to accommodate the coming-to-be of the mental. Certainly a classic contrast to the life of the mind is the dead inanimacy of a stone, which only the most devotedly panpsychic would see as participating in the mental pole of experience. Crystalline solids are characterized by a definite and tightly-knit organization of atoms into the order of the atomic lattice, whose inflexibility is the source of the material's rigidity. Its static structure contrasts with the dynamic interplay of proteins in the biochemical dance of the living cell. There is a looseness about life. The metaphor of the dance of creation[10] succeeds in holding together the ideas of ordered pattern and flexible movement in a way which is congenial to the sort of understanding I am trying to pursue.

That understanding may find further support from consideration of how creative thought is related to the unconscious mind. There often seems to be a threefold pattern in the discovery of new insight: (i) an intense conscious engagement with the problem, which nevertheless fails to yield to this assault; (ii) a fallow period, in which the problem is let go underground into the unconscious mind; (iii) the sudden emergence into consciousness of the actual solution, sometimes articulated in great detail. I imagine we have all had experiences of this kind. They are the basis of the advice to those in perplexity to 'sleep on it'. There are stories which illustrate the fruitfulness of unconscious process to an astonishing degree. Jacques Hadamard[11] tells how the distinguished French mathematician Poincaré had been wrestling with a deep mathematical problem. It totally failed to yield to him and he decided to give it up and go away on holiday. As he was stepping on to the bus on the way to his vacation the solution to the problem sprang into his mind complete in every detail. I think there are grounds for supposing that the fertility of the unconscious mind lies in its greater flexibility, its freedom of association, compared with the more rigid processes of the conscious ego. If that is so it would illustrate how the openness of flexible pattern is the key to mental creativity. The most obvious way in which the brain appears to differ from an immense computer is in the extraordinarily high degree of interconnectivity between its elements. Within the complementarity of material and mental, that wealth of interconnectedness might be the counterpart of the creative flexibility of which we are speaking. The many branches of the neural network would bear some analogy to the bifurcations of unstable dynamical systems, which endow the latter with the ability to become.

Even if there is something in all this, it cannot be the whole story. The argument thus far has presented mind as the complementary pole of matter. While the discussion has been very far from thinking of mind as an epiphenomenon of matter, it nevertheless has inextricably linked the two, just as wave and particle are not to be divorced from each other in conventional quantum theory.[12] Yet we have good reason for supposing that there are inhabitants of the mental world which are not anchored in the material. The first candidates I would like to consider are the truths of mathematics. It is difficult to believe that they come into being with the action of the human mind that first thinks them. Rather their nature seems to be that of ever-existing realities which are discovered, but not constructed, by the explorations of the human mind. Basic to all mathematics are the concepts of set theory. The great mathematician and logician Kurt Gödel wrote of them:

> Despite their remoteness from sense experience, we do have something like a perception of the objects of set theory, as seen from the fact that the axioms force themselves upon us as being true. I don't see any reason why we should have less confidence in this kind of perception, i.e. in mathematical intuition, than in sense perception.[13]

He is asserting the existence of a noetic realm in which we can participate without having created it or being able to exhaust its content, in much the same way that we participate in the physical world. Perhaps our relation to this noetic world is rather like the way in which a particular diagrammatic representation of a theorem in geometry participates in that theorem without being either its origin or its full expression.

There is no reason to suppose that the austere abstractions of mathematics would be the only inhabitants of such a world of thought. We have access to many other forms of mental experience and so it is reasonable to suppose that the entities relevant to that wider experience would also form part of the noetic world. I am using mental in the widest possible sense to embrace also what in other terminology might be called the spiritual. There might be active intelligences in that noetic world, which traditionally we would call angels. There might be powerful symbols, the 'thrones or dominions or principalities or authorities' of Pauline thought,[14] or the archetypes that Jung discerned as active in the depths of the human psyche.[15] There might even, I suppose, be other entities which shared man's 'amphibious' complementarity in the world of matter, and so were able to act within that world, but which operated, not within localized bodies, but within whatever flexibility there might be in overall process. If there really is a Jungian synchronicity at work in the world (p. 56), then it might have just that character. If there really are morphogenetic fields,[16] or parapsychological phenomena, then perhaps they too find their place there. I do not want to make the noetic world a sort of ragbag for accommodating any odd notion that comes along and I do not wish to commit myself on these latter questions. Certainly if such influences are at work with consequences in the material world, then they must be open at that level to appropriate scientific investigation, just as we are. Moreover their link with the noetic world would imply that they must have a rationality about them which such investigation would reveal, though not necessarily a rationality of a type to be anticipated from the study of 'ordinary' phenomena. Be that as it may, I simply want now to try to do justice to what seems to me to be a fundamental human experience, namely that by our biologically evolved consciousness we participate in a realm of reality which has not come into being either with us or with the origination of the physical world in the big bang, but which has always been there.

'Platonism' I hear you say. Your tone of voice is probably kindly but pitying, for such ideas are unfashionable in a culture which finds it easy to take the material more seriously than the mental. The view I am advocating differs, however, in two important respects from classical Platonism. In the first place it in no way assigns a priority to the mental over the material. That would be as bad a mistake as its converse. Both mental and material share equally in reality and for 'amphibians' like ourselves they are complementary necessities. Perhaps we can go even further. I would argue that the mutuality of mental and material is relevant to the insights of quantum theory about the structure of the physical world. The material universe as we encounter it seems so clear and dependable. Yet at its constituent roots it dissolves into the cloudy and fitful world of quantum unpicturability. Heisenberg tells us of the particles that make up matter that if we know where they are, we do not know what they are doing; if we know what they are doing, we do not know where they are. Nevertheless physicists have been resistant (and rightly so, in my opinion)[17] to any suggestion that these elusive quarks, gluons and electrons are simply convenient manners of speaking, as the positivists would allege. They are part of what *is*. I believe that if we are to defend the reality of elementary particles it is to their intelligibility that we shall have to appeal for the grounds of that defence. It is because they enable us to make sense of the world that we believe in them. We could say that we are convinced of the physical reality of the constituents of matter because they participate in that reality of understanding which characterizes the noetic world. In that sense alone I can see that there is a truth lying behind the otherwise implausible notions of panpsychism.

The second difference between what I am trying to say and the ideas of classical Platonism lies in the nature of the noetic world. It may be an everlasting world, containing truth not subject to change with time, but it is not an eternal uncreated world. It does not stand alongside God on equal terms but it depends upon him. I have said earlier (p. 51) that by such talk I do not wish to suggest that God is an intellectual tyrant, arbitrarily capable of manipulating the truths of mathematics. Those truths possess their certainty, not because they are the decrees of God's whimsical but unopposable will, but because they are let be by the One who is Reason itself and so incapable of irrationality.

The dependence of the noetic world on God is one of a number of differences between these ideas and some notions developed by Karl Popper.[18] He takes a pluralist view of reality, distinguishing between

> first, the world of physical objects or of physical states; secondly, the world of states of consciousness, or of mental states, or perhaps of behavioural dispositions to act; and, thirdly, the world of *objective contents of thought*, especially of scientific and poetic thoughts and works of art.[19]

Elsewhere he describes his World 3 as 'the world of intelligibles, or of *ideas in the objective sense*; it is a world of possible objects of thought: the world of theories in themselves, and their logical relations; of arguments in themselves; and of problem situations in themselves'.[20] Popper's excessively intellectualist approach to the understanding of everything makes these two definitions of World 3 not as different in his eyes as they might appear to others, who would question the implied equation of art and argument. His devaluation of intuition and tacit skills threatens to reduce poetry and art to the consideration of problem situations. He regards his third world as 'a natural product of the human mind, comparable to a spider's web',[21] but yet he insists that it is also autonomous. This ambiguous character is scarcely made clearer by his claim that the natural numbers (the integers) are the work of man but that their properties of oddness and evenness, and of being prime, illustrate the autonomy of such a human artefact. It is the sense we have of discovering mathematical properties, such as primeness, which Popper believes sustains this claim to autonomy. But would it not be equally true to say the same of the discovery of the integers themselves, which Kronecker said were the work of God?

World 3 contains not only true ideas but also false ones. Indeed it must be pretty well silted up with the latter, since for each true statement such as $2+2=4$ there is an infinity of false statements of the form $2+2=n$, where n is any number other than 4. Popper's three worlds interact and World 2 is the mediator of the interaction between Worlds 1 and 3, since consciousness has access both to the objects of thought and to the objects of the physical world. In a very crude translation between Popper's picture and mine, one might say that I see 'World 2' as the region of complementary overlap between 'Worlds 1 and 3'. We have seen how the possibility of that complementarity might indeed arise from an indefiniteness lying, in Popper's phrase, between the order of clocks and the disorder of clouds. Since there are certainly mistaken thoughts, I suppose I must admit that there are false ideas in 'World 3', though I think it would be right to distinguish that subset of the noetic world populated by true ideas as being the higher reality. (Is there scope for borrowing from the perennial philosophy's theory of 'evil as non-being' and thinking of error as the privation of the truth?) I cannot find myself persuaded by the idea of World 3 as a human cultural deposit evolving a life of its own, but instead I wish to look to God as the Creator of the noetic world. Consequently it is to a theologian that I have to turn for help.

Jürgen Moltmann has some interesting things to say which seem to me to bear some relation to these ideas, though again expressed in a different way. He endeavours to take seriously the confession of the Creed that God is the Creator of 'heaven and earth'.[22] In relation to creation understood as an open system he defines these terms by saying 'We call the determined side of this system "earth", the undetermined side "heaven"' and he goes on to speak of heaven as 'a finite but immortal creation, while earth can be seen as a finite and transitory creation'. A world without heaven 'would be a closed system, resting and revolving within itself'.[23] I am not sure where mathematics comes in Moltmann's scheme of things but at least his emphasis on openness accords with what I have been saying about the relationship of the mental to the material, namely that it involves a degree of indefiniteness of organization, an indefiniteness which Prigogine has taught us is connected with the possibility of becoming and so with the realization of potentiality. There is clearly some consonance between aspects of the noetic world of which I am speaking and Moltmann's created heaven. He goes on to say that the symbol 'heaven' describes 'the potentialities and potencies of God' but they are not

the potentialities and potencies of his eternal essence *per se*. They are the potentialities and potencies of the God who has designated himself to be the Creator of a world different from himself, which none the less communicates with him . . . the divine potentialities and potencies described in the term 'heaven' are qualified through God's designation of himself to be Creator; and they are unfolded and disclosed by the Creator in the time and in the space of creation.

In this respect heaven is the first world which God created so that from there he might form the earth, encompass it, and finally redeem it.[24]

This reminds us of two important facts. My talk about the noetic world has been strongly intellectualist in tone, influenced by my point of entry into it through the truths of mathematics. 'The potentialities and potencies of God' are not so limited. He is very much more than just the Great Mathematician. Just as the Platonic world contains both forms of truth and forms of beauty, integrated in the form of the good, so the noetic world of which I am trying to speak will include, along with mathematical truth, aesthetic and moral truth, integrated in love. Also, the scope of the creative activity of the 'potentialities and potencies of God' is not to be limited to the readily discernible regularities of common occurrence. Nothing I am saying denies the possibility that God's relationship with his creation exhibits particular aspects in particular circumstances. What is conventionally called the miraculous is coherent within the picture here presented, provided it is understood – as surely theologically it must be understood – as a sign of a deeper rationality underlying the whole, rather than as a divine *tour de force* bearing an arbitrary relation to the rest of the world's process. The possibility of miracle is part of the openness of creation to its Creator, who in his steadfast love is neither tyrannical nor indifferent.

We have to bear all this in mind when we take account of the second fact of which Moltmann reminds us. God himself is not to be found in that noetic world. At best it contains his energies (as the Eastern theologians would say) but not his essence; it is part of his creative act but not of his very self. Moltmann warns us of the dangers of failing to distinguish God and heaven: 'The fulfiller of hope is equated with hope's fulfilment. The fulfiller no longer transcends the fulfilment of the desire which he himself awakens. So God is turned into the fulfilment of the wish projections of human beings.'[25] Confusing God with his creation ultimately replaces theology with anthropology, in the manner of Feuerbach. The Christian understanding is stated by St John of Damascus when he writes: 'God does not belong to the class of existing things: not that he has no existence, but he is above all existing things, nay even above existence itself.'[26]

Mathematics can offer us a parabolic way of thinking about the God who lies beyond the world of his creation. The non-mathematical may feel surprised at this but their astonishment will abate when they learn that the insight arises from mathematical exploration of the idea of infinity.

Numbers go on for ever; however big a number you choose to think of I can always outbid you by adding to it. Thus crudely thought of, infinity might appear to be nothing more than the incomparably big 'number' at the inaccessible end of the mathematical line. It was a capital discovery by Georg Cantor in the late nineteenth century that there was very much more to be said than that. He discovered the modern theory of transfinite numbers which gives an account of the structured hierarchy of types of infinity, each characterized by the appropriate cardinal number.[27] Lowest in that hierarchy is the countable infinity corresponding to the possibility of an endless enumeration (1, 2, 3 . . . world without end), whose cardinal is called *aleph zero*. If you ask how many rational numbers (that is, fractions) there are between 0 and 1, then the answer is *aleph zero* since you can count them in a sequence (such as 1/2, 1/3, 2/3, 1/4, 3/4, 1/5 . . . where I am using an obvious ordering principle). However the real numbers (that is, all decimals, recurring or non-recurring) lying between 0 and 1 are too numerous to be counted off in this way. Beyond *aleph zero* lies an endlessly increasing sequence of cardinal numbers, each specifying a further order of infinity. And beyond that? The set theorists have found it useful to define the Absolute Infinity, lying beyond the sequence of transfinite cardinals, to which they have assigned the ultimate symbol, Ω. The concept of Ω is meaningful to set theorists, though it is also inconceivable in the sense that Ω eludes all attempts at precise definition. Rucker says 'For "Ω is inconceivable" is the same as "there is no conceivable property P that uniquely characterizes Ω"'.[28] One might almost speak of apophatic mathematics! Rucker twists that metaphor round and says 'set theory could be viewed as a form of exact theology'.[29] Analogy is the method of theology and the ineffable Ω can serve as an aid to thought about the God beyond the complexity of his creation. Pursuing that analogy too far, however, may lead us into perplexity and error. 'Whenever P is a conceivable property of Ω, then there must be other ordinals also enjoying property P.'[30] Applying that idea to theology would lead to something like emanationism, a trailing off of the divine in the direction of creation. The noetic world would become a gnostic pleroma filled with all sorts of curious semi-divine entities.[31] Analogies always have their limitations.

Mathematics is part of the noetic world. In a remarkable way it illustrates the openness of that world which Moltmann sees as the characterizing property of created heaven. Gödel showed that every mathematical system which includes arithmetic (that is to say, has a structure sufficiently complicated to accommodate the whole numbers) contains statements which are stateable but not decidable within that system. Truth always exceeds what can be proved. Rucker comments on this: 'Try to catch the universe in a finite net of axioms and the universe will fight back. Reality is, on the deepest level, essentially infinite. No finitely programmed machine can ever exhaust the richness of the mental and physical world we inhabit.'[32] There are realities which elude confinement in our limited minds. The set theorists cannot catch Ω in their axiomatic net but it is a concept open to their intuition. God too escapes our grasp but not our worship. 'By love he can be caught and held but by thinking never.'[33] Rowan Williams speaks of the moment of spiritual illumination as 'the running out of language and thought, the compulsion exercised by a reality drastically and totally beyond the reach of our conceptual apparatus.'[34]

That is no bad point at which to try to gather our thoughts together. There is a paradoxical clash between the ambitiously all-embracing title of this chapter and its modest content. The grandeur of the theme contrasts with the paucity of our comprehension. I am groping for an understanding which does justice both to what science can tell us about the world and also to our experience of a much wider reality than that which science could ever claim to explain. Those who fail to take the latter into account end up with a stunted story, sterilely implausible in its diminished scope.[35] Those who take insufficient account of scientific insight are neglecting an essential source of understanding. Curiously enough, they seem to me to include among their number some who purport to use science as a guide in their metaphysical construction. Whitehead's view of reality as a concatenation of events is sometimes thought to be supported by modern quantum theory. I think that is only superficially so. The continuity of development of the wavefunction between acts of measurement, and the conservation laws of elementary particle physics preserving aspects of the situation, indicate to me that the enduring concept of entity is not to be abandoned in favour of the punctuated concept of event. Talk of quarks and electrons is still indispensably fundamental.

I have similar reservations about the ideas of David Bohm. He has made very enlightening contributions to quantum physics but his wider thought seems to me to take off into flights of speculative fancy which are evocative rather than explanatory. Concerning his idea of holomovement he says:

> A new notion of order is involved here, which we called the *implicate order* . . . In terms of the implicate order one may say that everything is enfolded into everything. This contrasts with the *explicate order* now dominant in physics in which things are *unfolded* in the sense that each thing lies only in its own particular region of space (and time) and outside the regions belonging to other things.[36]

He has some interesting parables about what an implicate order might mean, such as the hologram which encodes in every spot information about the whole of its object. The idea also bears some relation to Bohm's causal version of quantum theory. In this brilliant and instructive counter to conventional quantum mechanics, Bohm proposed a divorce between wave and particle. The particle is what we see; the wave is a 'pilot' wave, carrying information about the environment, and manifesting itself solely by its guidance of the particle. Particles would thus be members of the explicate order in their separate identities. The wave enfolds knowledge of the whole and so partakes of the implicate order. Most physicists have found Bohm's ingenious theory to be too contrived to carry conviction. The wider notion of holomovement, in any case, requires considerable elaboration beyond its quantum mechanical beginnings and I see it more as a vision of wholeness (which I wish to share) rather than as an aid to understanding what is (which I am also seeking).

Beside the baroque grandeurs of process philosophy or holomovement, all I can set is the humble picture of material/mental complementarity by which the physical world participates in a wider noetic world, all being held in being by the creative will of God.[37] But then I have always preferred a hut on the ground to a castle in the sky.

6

Theological Science

One whose habits of thought have been formed by the practice of science will approach the consideration of wider questions from a point of view necessarily influenced by his experience. This imposition of an intellectual perspective is a source of both limitation and insight. We must have somewhere to stand when we survey the world, but we must bear in mind the possibility that our vantage point obscures from us important features of the scene which others will more readily discern. The scientist – perhaps particularly one who has worked in the abstract austerity of fundamental physics – will realize that his professional expertise qualifies him only to pronounce on a limited range of issues. Yet when his search for understanding carries him beyond the area of his technical competence, as necessarily it will, his intellectual instincts may still have some value as one way of approaching the deeper reality he is seeking to explore. Mathematicians who think about multidimensional entities sometimes aid their thoughts by surveying a selection of computer-generated three-dimensional sections, which are themselves displayed as perspectives on a two-dimensional video screen. Each of these sections has something true to say about the original object, though each is only a very restricted account of one aspect of it. Above all other disciplines of intellectual inquiry, theology needs the help of many perspectives in framing its account of 'infinite-dimensional' reality. The habits of thought of the scientist may provide their own modest input to that great endeavour. I want, therefore, to try to sketch something of a scientist's approach to theology.

The title of this chapter is also the title of a well-known book by the Scottish systematic theologian, Thomas Torrance.[1] He is one of the few contemporary British theologians to take a serious interest in scientific matters, though his great heroes, Maxwell and Einstein, are figures of the final flowering of classical physics rather than to be found among the creators of the new world view that quantum theory brought about.[2] It is perhaps not surprising that Torrance's theological writings lay great emphasis on the givenness, indeed the objectivity, of God. Speaking of theological inquiry, he writes: 'The primary thing we have to note is the utter lordship of the Object, its absolute precedence, for that is the one all-determining presupposition of theology.'[3] It is, of course, congenial to the scientific mind to recognize that our search for truth about the world includes response to a reality standing over against us, whose idiosyncratic nature we must respect and which tempers and restrains our speculative flights of fancy. Elsewhere Torrance warns us that when

> thought and reality part company, the world becomes opaque and meaningless no matter how coherent the clear and distinct ideas we have generated, for the more man tries to force clear-cut meaning of his own devising upon the world, the more he cuts himself off from nature and is apt to misuse it for his own ends.[4]

The very transition from the naively objective world, as perceived by Newton and Maxwell, to the elusive quantum world of Heisenberg and Dirac is a tale of the often reluctant recognition by physicists of the strangeness of what actually *is*.[5] If encounter with the physical world can so sharply revise our understanding of what rationally can be said about its nature, it would scarcely be surprising if the pursuit of the divine required openness to the unexpected. It is the essence of scientific investigation to seek to conform thought to the nature of its object, as encountered in its interaction with us. Understood in this sense, theological science lies at the heart of faith's search for understanding.

Torrance claims that modern theology in its distinctive form began with John Calvin, who started his discussion, not with speculative essence but with experienced actuality. The fundamental theological question posed by Calvin is said to be: 'What is the nature of the thing we have here?'[6] Torrance goes on to quote with approval John Murray's remark, 'Reason is the capacity to behave in terms of the nature of the object'.[7] Such an attitude is one that a scientist instinctively shares and applauds.

Conformity to the object takes one form in physical science, where we transcend the natural world and have power to put it to the test. It takes an entirely different form in theology, where the Object of our inquiry transcends us and where 'You shall not put the Lord your God to the test'[8] is a fundamental law of the spiritual life. Torrance says:

> It is because we come to know God in His transcendental Majesty and Truth, and know Him to be greater than we can ever conceive or express, that we acknowledge the limitation and relativity of all our forms of thought and speech about Him. Theological knowledge is thus profoundly relative because it is relative to the Absolute, and profoundly objective because it has for its primary Object God who can only be known through Himself and not by reference beyond Him.[9]

However valuable natural theology may be in pointing to the divine and affording insight into his creation, it will only at best be able by itself to bring us to the Cosmic Architect or Great Mathematician. The God and Father of our Lord Jesus Christ is to be sought by other means. Worship and prayer is the context in which theology has to be practised; the academic departments of religious studies in our universities are like schools of science unfurnished with laboratories. As Macquarrie says, 'Who ever addressed a prayer to a necessary being?'[10] Many of the Fathers of the early Church lived as monks, so that their thought was grounded in the practice of the religious life. Commenting on the great symbol of the Word, the Father's eternal utterance, Torrance says, 'theological thinking is more listening than any other form of knowledge'.[11] There is a degree of impassivity about it. So much of the initiative lies elsewhere than in ourselves. Hence the use of the word 'revelation' by theology. Torrance also points us to the 'epistemological inversion' involved in the recognition that the One we seek to know already knows us through and through.[12]

Theology shares the lack of power to manipulate and interrogate its material with all other forms of intrinsically personal knowledge. This contrasts with the power of testing inquiry possessed by the impersonal mode of scientific investigation. As a theoretical physicist I gladly acknowledge the indispensable role of experiment in my subject. It is this that gives science its ability to settle questions to universal satisfaction. To be sure, such activity is not wholly free from the exercise of tacit skills of personal judgement about significance and relevance and choice of line of attack,[13] but it is relatively free compared to other forms of human inquiry. In the realms of more highly personal knowledge, such a degree of intersubjective agreement as science enjoys is not available. Yet to suppose that fact to mean that truth is not to be found in these other disciplines would be a gravely diminishing stance to adopt.

Another power we lose in personal encounter is the ability to predict. Only in the event itself is its meaning to be found. It cannot be laid down beforehand nor prescribed by those who are merely observers and not participants. The religious believer is ill and prays for the gift of wholeness in the experience. He may find it in physical recovery or in the acceptance of disability or death. What will happen to him cannot be predicted, nor may any but he say whether the experience, when it comes, is one of wholeness or of disintegration.

Scientific knowledge is concerned with generalities, what all can find if they choose to look. In consequence it has a repeatable, and so shareable, character to it. Personal encounter is always idiosyncratic, because each individual is unique. We may find analogies in the experience of others but never identity. We all hear a Beethoven quartet differently, and we ourselves never quite hear it in the same way twice. Hence the scandal of particularity, which for Christian theology finds its most startling exemplification in the unique status claimed for Jesus Christ. While such a claim clearly calls for the most careful assessment, it is a rational possibility in the sphere of the personal that God should have made himself uniquely known in a particular man.

Some of the contrasts that are made between science and theology, however, are ill-founded. Theissen,[14] for example, has propounded 'three contradictions between scientific thought and faith' to which he appears to accord at least partial endorsement, but with which I disagree. They are:

(i) 'Hypothetical scientific thought versus apodeictic faith': Science is always trying out things to see if they are true, whilst faith simply asserts 'a truth from which we cannot withdraw under any conditions'.

On the contrary, I believe theology to be corrigible, knowing that every image of God is ultimately an idol.

(ii) 'Scientific thought is subject to falsification; faith goes against the facts.'

Of course the personal facts of faith are more subtle to assess than those of science, as we have just been acknowledging, but we are certainly not called to believe whatever the evidence against that belief. Equally the falsifiability of a general scientific view is a delicate matter. It does not crumble at the first apparently adverse result, for phenomena are never so tidy as to fit perfectly what is proposed. Judgement is need to decide whether a discrepancy is serious or venial. When Einstein was told in 1921 that Miller had measured a non-zero aether drift (which would have contradicted Special Relativity) he serenely replied, 'Subtle is the Lord but malicious He is not!'[15] His confidence in his theory proved justified, though why Miller got the results he did has never been fully explained.

(iii) 'Scientific thought delights in dissension; faith is based on consensus.'

If scientists were always questioning received results the subject would be an unfruitful chaos. In fact they usually find it very difficult to accept radical change of view, even when it appears forced upon them by phenomena. The tale of the discovery of parity non-conservation (that there is an intrinsic 'handedness' in fundamental physics) is a long story of theorists and experimenters alike averting their attention from a dissenting possibility, until Lee and Yang had the intellectual courage to grasp that particular nettle.[16] On the other side, the history of religion is full of the influence of prophet and reformer who have proclaimed an unwelcome insight contrary to general expectation.

These three contradictions which Theissen so starkly proposes are false oppositions and do not call for his ingenious but unconvincing theory that they represent respectively (i) 'different forms of adapting to unknown reality'; (ii) 'different forms of coping with the pressures of selection exercised by reality'; (iii) 'different forms of the openness of our spiritual life to mutations' in the evolutionary history of culture.[17] That is not to deny that religious experience (i) involves a greater degree of personal commitment than science; (ii) deals with aspects of reality which are not to be manipulated in the way that science can submit its phenomena to the experimental test; (iii) looks to the collective experience of the community of faith as one norm against which to assess the validity of individual insight. The differences between science and theology are neither to be glossed over nor exaggerated to the point of complete disjunction.

They share a comradely concern in the search for truth about the world. They are, therefore, both parts of *scientia* in its medieval sense of 'knowledge'. Whether they are both to be incorporated within some cleverly chosen modern definition of science is a semantic question about which we do not need to get unduly excited. After all, 'scientific' is a cachet of real but limited value. 'Rational' is the epithet truly to be desirable and to this theology can lay justifiable claim, as it seeks 'to behave in terms of the nature of the object'.

The diverse natures of our encounter with the world are no reason for not trying to seek a unity of knowledge about it. Indeed in Chapter 2 we argued that the quest for understanding through and through is ultimately a search for the one true God. His reason is the ground of the pattern and structure of the physical world, his joy the ground of our experience of beauty, his will the ground of moral imperative, and his presence the ground of prayer and worship. The coherence of theism lies in its synoptic explanatory power, its ability to hold together the variety of our experience. Theology may represent one end of a spectrum of human knowledge, ranging from relatively impersonal science through personal encounter to the numinous presence of the One who transcends personality, but it is part of one great rational inquiry into the way things are. I have great sympathy with Austin Farrer when he writes: 'The mysteries of faith must fit into one universe of sense with our natural knowledge of human personality, of history, of the form of nature, of the principles of being; if they did not, they would not continue to be believed.'[18] He is writing within a tradition which wishes to make a distinction between natural and supernatural, which I myself would not wish to draw. Nevertheless he acknowledges that 'Supernatural revelation extends the natural power of this faculty [understanding], it does not distort or supplant it.'[19] That being so it seems to me that the distinction is one that it is not helpful to make; natural and supernatural are simply ways of speaking about different levels in the one rationality, whose seamless character is a reflection of the oneness of the Creator and of his consistency in relation to the world.

Those who speak of the unity of knowledge will still wish to respect the insights of the different disciplines when they speak of those aspects of experience which are the proper objects of their study. It is a unity to be achieved by the search for synthesis, rather than by reduction to a falsely simplified common denominator. Intellectual take-over bids, such as sociobiology's claim to reduce social and ethical matters to the issue of genetic survival (leading to 'Pangloss made scientific through the agency of Charles Darwin', as has wittily been said),[20] will be seen to be what they are, Procrustean imposures of great implausibility. The inescapably personal character of knowledge will be respected and we shall not give way to 'a passion for achieving absolutely impersonal knowledge which, being unable to recognize any persons, presents us with a picture of the universe in which we ourselves are absent.'[21]

Part of the web of personal experience is that claim to encounter with the ground of being, the assurance of meaningfulness, the focus of hope, which we call experience of the presence of God. Swinburne has given a careful discussion of its evidential value.[22] He enunciates Principles of Credulity and of Testimony, which may be summed up by adopting, as a reasonable initial stance, the maxim, 'How things seem to be is good grounds for belief about how they are.' Of course, there are difficulties in applying this dictum to religious experience, both because that experience is reported in such apparently different terms by the plurality of the world's religions, and also because, though it is more widespread even in the sceptically inclined western world than we are often liable to suppose,[23] there are certainly people who would deny they had any access to it whatsoever.

The testimony of the tone deaf would not be allowed to negate the reality of music and so it seems reasonable that those who claim never to have had a sense of the divine should not be given equal weight with those (the majority in the history of mankind) who have. Even in science we are aware that our seeing of the world is always seeing-as, our vision is refracted by those 'spectacles behind the eyes' imposed by our theoretical preconceptions.[24] In the personal domain the perspectives of culture play a more dominant role and this may go far (but perhaps not all the way) to explain why the world's religions do not speak with one voice.

Christianity differs from the other world religions most sharply in the claim it makes for the unique status of God-man for Jesus Christ. It is beyond the scope of this book to attempt to assess that claim in any detail.[25] Our present concern is with the attitude which informs such attempts and which I believe bears some analogy to science's stance in its exploration of the physical world. That stance is characterized by a willingness to allow the phenomena to set the terms of attainable understanding, a refusal to impose an a priori notion of what is reasonable, but to seek, rather, to respond to what actually appears to be the case. The rationality we seek is one conformed to 'the nature of the object'. The spirit of the search is exactly contrary to the procedure described by John Macquarrie when he wrote:

> If someone asks whether unicorns exist . . . One would first of all consult zoologists and ask whether a unicorn is a conceivable form of life. It might turn out that there was nothing biologically impossible about a unicorn. Then one would institute a search for an actual specimen.[26]

Admittedly Macquarrie says that such a mode of inquiry would not suit natural theology, and the reason he gives is that God is not an object among objects. But it wouldn't suit zoology either, for it greatly overestimates the previsionary powers of zoologists. When scientists become confident that they know what is possibly what, they make the most awful mistakes. For a hundred years the medical profession refused to take account of the many operations performed painlessly under a mesmeric trance because hypnosis found no place in its scheme of things.

As an example of what such openness to the nature of the object might mean, let us consider Christology, the attempt – central to all Christian thinking – to come to a just understanding of the event of Jesus Christ. Our first task will have to be to consider what it is that we need to explain. From this point of view, it is necessarily the work of Christ which forms the starting point for christological exploration and which constrains possible theories of the nature of Christ. That way we start by establishing the character of the phenomena we are attempting to understand. The witness of the New Testament is to a great saving act of God in Jesus which has opened up new and transforming hope for mankind:

> Therefore, if any one is in Christ, he is a new creation; the old has passed away, behold, the new has come. All this is from God, who through Christ reconciled us to himself and gave us the ministry of reconciliation; that is, God was in Christ reconciling the world to himself, not counting their trespasses against them and entrusting to us the message of reconciliation.[27]

This is a dominant thought in Paul, who expresses it in his own particular way, but it is to be found in all the other major New Testament writers also.[28] The experience of salvation through Christ is one to which the Church has borne testimony down the ages. How we assess these claims will determine what it is that Christology has to explain. If one believes, as I do, that the New Testament writers are correct in their assertion that in Jesus a great act of divine reconciliation has taken place, which makes available to men a power to transform their lives which they could not have had of themselves alone, then what we believe about Jesus will have to be adequate to explain that fact. An evolutionary view of Jesus as the 'new emergent' in creation[29] fails that test, for what hope could such a figure provide for us who have not emerged? A similar difficulty confronts inspirational views of Christology,[30] which see the special character of Jesus as resulting from his being filled with a unique measure of the divine Spirit, a quantitative rather than a qualitative difference from other prophets and men of God. I personally do not perceive any view of Jesus' person which is capable of coping with these salvific claims about him, which does not seek to wrestle with two difficult and deeply mysterious assertions of orthodox Christian theology: the doctrine of the incarnation (that the hypostatic union of divine and human natures in Christ provides a unique meeting point between God and men through which divine saving power is made available to men – the divine assumption of total humanity to bring about its total redemption); the doctrine of the Body of Christ (which proclaims human solidarity in Christ, so that through that union the life of God is made available to all mankind). Of course, these are counter-intuitive notions which we have the greatest difficulty in grasping. Anyone whose habits of thought have been formed by the practice of science will recognize, if not always welcome, that the complex strangeness of the world can lead us into regimes which in their true nature run counter to the intuitions of everyday life. If science does nothing else it ought to liberate us from an undue tyranny of common sense. The duality of God and man in Christ is a perplexing matter. So is the duality of wave and particle with which quantum theory has made us familiar. The solidarity of mankind in sin and salvation is equally perplexing. So is the 'togetherness in separation' which Einstein, Podolsky and Rosen discovered to be a consequence of quantum theory.[31] The latter asserts that once two quantum mechanical entities, such as two electrons, have interacted with each other, they retain the power of mutual influence however far they may subsequently separate from each other. Wave/particle duality and the EPR phenomenon have received convincing endorsement from our experimental investigation of the physical world. The doctrines of the incarnation and of the Body of Christ equally arose as responses to Christian experience. They were not flights of ungrounded speculation. Of course, their adequate discussion calls for more space and much more learning than I have at my disposal. This brief account is simply to suggest that in a rational inquiry, or theological science rightly so called, these doctrines are motivated by a desire to understand what actually is the case. That is the basis of the comradeship of theology and natural science. I am not seeking to produce a modern bestiary in which I look at an electron and think of Christ. Even less do I want to suggest that in some way the peculiarities of quantum theory explain the peculiarities of divinity. Each testifies to the rich idiosyncrasy of its own subject. Ian Ramsey said of the logic of theology that, even if it 'is not identical with that of poetry, it is sufficiently like it in being odd'.[32] One might say the same of quantum logic.[33] Oddness (a favourite Ramsey word) betokens the surprising peculiarity of the way things are and, consequently, of how we must speak of them.

It is this attempt to respond to the complexity of our experience which appears to me (to the small extent that I understand matters of comparative religion) to be more successfully pursued by the religions of the Near East than by those of the Far East. The great Near Eastern religions, Judaism, Christianity and Islam, seem to take the reality of the world more seriously than the religions of the Far East, which discern in its processes the play of illusion. Fritjof Capra[34] has claimed that the elusive world of quantum fields in interaction corresponds more sympathetically to the dancing, dissolving yet unified, world of eastern thought, than to the realistically conceived world of the West. It is a half-truth. Though the physical world has a subtler reality than that of naive objectivity, it has its own form of persistent rationality which we must respect and which is the ultimate guarantee of its reality.[35] We can illustrate this by reference to Capra's own arguments. Writing in 1975 he still clung to a 'dissolving' view of the constituents of matter called the bootstrap (p. 10). This supposed that there were no fundamental constituents, everything being made of everything else. Over against that was the opposing possibility that there are fundamental constituents of matter (the quarks and gluons) whose properties would be manifested by the symmetrical relationships they would imply amongst the observed particles which were made out of them. Capra saw such notions of symmetry as an out-dated remnant of Greek thought which the traditions of the East would reject, since for them: 'the concept of symmetry does not seem to play any major role in their philosophy. Like geometry, it is thought to be a construct of the mind, rather than a property of nature, and thus of no fundamental importance.'[36] To speak thus slightingly of the role of symmetry in particle physics was already pretty odd in 1975. Since then the great advances in the subject have all come from exploitation of the insight of symmetry. This story shows us the way in which we need continually to be open to 'the capacity to behave in terms of the nature of the object', whatever that nature may prove to be.

Theology faces a particular difficulty in that the nature of its Object transcends us and our power to grasp him. We do not have the words and concepts with which to encapsulate God. Inescapably we are driven to the use of analogy. No doubt words such as personal, loving, beautiful, are used of God by extension from our human experience, but they are surely used as extensions in the right direction. As Augustine said of the Holy Trinity, we speak of such things because it is better than to be totally silent. Thus it comes about that the language of theology is the language of symbol. Symbols, whether verbal (as in poem or story) or sensual (as in art or music) have an openness which refuses to tie down that to which they refer but rather makes it available to individual response and apprehension. The literary critic, Northrop Frye, writing about the Bible, says that it 'belongs to an area of language in which metaphor is functional and where we have to surrender precision to flexibility'.[37] The scientist may feel uncomfortable with that, until he realizes that it is a proper recognition of the nature of the Object with which we have to do.

Symbol involves a dialectical interplay between representation and interpretation. The point of focus is provided by the carrier of the symbol – the poem or the picture – but it is the surrounding cloud of allusion and suggestion which creates in the participant his individual act of understanding. The great Christian symbols are located in history; their focus is on events in the life of Israel and the Church and upon the great event of the life, death and resurrection of Jesus Christ. Because of that, Christianity is anchored in history just as physics is anchored in physical phenomena. But it transcends history, just as physics transcends the merely phenomenological, by seeking to find what is happening in what is going on. Both poles of the dialectic, representation and interpretation, event and image, are essential. Farrer says: 'Certainly the events without the images would be no revelation at all, and the images without the events would remain shadows on the clouds.'[38] They have to be held together, interacting with each other, but neither being reduced to an epiphenomenon of the other, just as theoretical and experimental insights coexist in physics. Theories are not just convenient summaries of data (as the positivists wrongly allege) nor are they the imposition of man-made patterns on apparently plastic phenomena (as the idealists wrongly allege). It is in the synthesis of creative exploration by the mind and respect for accounts of how things actually are, that physical truth is to be sought and found.

Natural science does enjoy the exercise of procedures for testing its insights. They are impossible to specify in exact detail – claims of simple verifiability or falsifiability oversimplify the matter by discounting the tacit skills required to decide when a discrepancy is significant or is venial – but there is a recognizable, if not exhaustively characterizable, way in which phenomena control theories. Hence the impressive, experimentally-led, character of the advance of scientific knowledge.

Because of the more highly personal nature of its phenomena and the role that flexible symbol, rather than precise mathematics, plays in its discourse, theology cannot be expected to achieve the same agreed and cumulative character. Nevertheless it would be disconcerting, and destructive of any claim to be called theological science, if it did not display in its procedures an openness of response to the way things are. Ian Barbour says that 'The key question is whether in religion *the data exercise any control at all* on the interpretation.'[39] I have already indicated that I think they do. Believers are not in the business of shutting their eyes, gritting their teeth, and committing themselves to irrational assertions. I agree with Barbour when he goes on to say: 'In my view God is known through interpreted experience of three kinds:

religious experience, patterns of the world and particular historical events.'[40] This threefold appeal to tradition (including our own contribution to its accumulation of experience), reason (including natural theology's contribution to the rational exploration of the world) and Scripture (recording historical events of particular significance, including the event of Jesus Christ) provides the tripodal basis for theological science's inquiry. The Greek Fathers spoke of a threefold embodiment of divine reason: in the *logoi* of things in creation, the *logoi* of Scripture and the *Logos* made flesh, a similar, if somewhat differently organized, triad of testimony. Scripture has a more profound aspect than simply that of being the record of 'particular historical events'. It is certainly to be read in that mode and when we do so we should exercise all the scholarly skills at our disposal in order to assess it as evidence. But there is also a meditative way of reading (the *lectio divina* of monasticism) in which we allow it to dissolve in our minds and we submit ourselves to its authority. Here Scripture and experience blend. The Bible is then treated as God's word, not in the sense of its being a divinely dictated and guaranteed answer to everything, but as the inspired writings which continue to act as vehicles of the Spirit. We are back to the role that listening must play in theological inquiry. The thrust of the new canonical criticism[41] is to try to do justice to this part that Scripture has played in the continuing life of the Church.

The test of the validity of the exercise of theological investigation will lie in its ability to discern pattern, to offer coherent understanding of human experience at its most profound. The insight that it affords into the way things are is the criterion of theology's success in responding to Reality. For the Christian, the centre of that insight lies in the pattern of death and resurrection, given in the life of Jesus Christ, and disclosing to us what lies at the heart of divine reality. The incarnation is not only the meeting point of God and man, it is also the complete fusion of event and image, the perfect symbol integrating representation and interpretation. The delicate and dangerous word 'myth' cannot be done without in this discourse. Its use is not a circumspect way of hinting that one is dealing with ungrounded constructions of the imagination – in short, with untruths. Quite the contrary. Myth is concerned with conveying truth so deep that only story can afford the appropriate vehicle. The narrative of Adam and

Eve and the fatal plucking of the apple, leading to their expulsion from paradise, is freed to perform its proper purpose when it is recognized as an ever-contemporary picture of alienation from God, rather than an account of a primeval disaster. In this way the story addresses deep levels and needs within us, which would be untouched by articulated psychological or theological discussion. The peculiar force of myth explains why the symbols of Adam and Eve and the serpent fascinate us still. Yet there is another peculiar force in the story that we know to be a true account of what actually happened. When we read of heroic fortitude in the concentration camps of World War II, what moves us is the thought that it was actual men and women, ostensibly like ourselves, who endured such things with such courage.

The power of myth and the power of actuality fuse in the incarnation. What could be more profound than that God should take human form, make himself known in human terms, share the suffering of the strange world he has made and on the cross open his arms to embrace its bitterness? That is a story which moves me at the deepest possible level. Yet it is no tale projected on to a shadowy figure of ancient legend. It is concerned with what actually happened in the concrete person of Jesus Christ, a wandering teacher in a particular province of the Roman Empire, at a particular point in history. The centre of Christianity lies in the *realized myth* of the incarnation. Theological science is based on the encounter with the Jesus Christ in whom we are confronted with 'a complex fact *that includes its own interpretation as part of its own facticity*'[42] because, as St John tells us, 'the Word became flesh and dwelt among us, full of grace and truth; we have beheld his glory, glory as of the only Son from the Father'.[43]

We have come to the end of our discussion. In its course, science and theology have encountered each other in a way that seems, to me at least, to be characterized by fruitful interaction rather than mutual friction. Einstein once said, 'Religion without science is blind. Science without religion is lame'.[44] His instinct that they need each other was right, though I would not describe their separate shortcomings in quite the terms he chose. Rather I would say, 'Religion without science is confined; it fails to be completely open to reality. Science without religion is incomplete; it fails to attain the deepest possible understanding.' The remarkable insights that science affords us into the intelligible workings of the world cry out for an explanation more profound than that which it itself can provide. Religion, if it is to take seriously its claim that the world is the creation of God, must be humble enough to learn from science what that world is actually like. The dialogue between them can only be mutually enriching. The scientist will find in theology a unifying principle more fundamental than the grandest unified field theory. The theologian will encounter in science's account of the pattern and structure of the physical world a reality which calls forth his admiration and wonder. Together they can say with the psalmist:

O Lord how manifold are thy works!
In wisdom thou hast made them all.[45]

NOTES

Introduction

1 Polkinghorne (1979), pp. 43–4.
2 Quoted in Torrance (1969), p. 12.

Chapter 1 Natural Theology

1 Moltmann (1985). For example, Chapter 6 discusses space without mentioning General Relativity.
2 Barth (1949), p. 23.
3 Montefiore (1985), pp. 3–4.
4 von Rad (1972), p. 199.
5 Prov. 14.20.
6 Prov. 17.27.
7 von Rad (1975), p. 448.
8 Prov. 21.30.
9 1 Kings 4.29–34.
10 Ecclus. 24.8.
11 Job 40.15.
12 Moltmann (1985), p. 36.
13 Prov. 30.18–19.
14 Prov. 8.22–6.
15 Ecclus. 24.3; presumably alluding to Gen. 1 and 2 (thus Snaith (1974), p. 121, though the Greek of Ecclesiasticus has no exact verbal parallels with the Septuagint of Genesis).
16 Prov. 8.30–1.
17 von Rad (1972), p. 163.
18 John 1.1–14.
19 Ps. 33.6.
20 Col. 1.17. The verb is *sunestēmi*, a standing together.
21 Rom. 1.20.
22 Wiles (1966), p. 27.
23 Augustine, *Commentary on John*, 29.6.

24 For example, under addition modulo 1000.

25 For further discussion see e.g. B. Davies (1982), ch. 4. Ward (1982, p. 30) claims that the ontological argument does contain reference to the state of the universe since the appeal to a maximally perfect being would make no sense if the world were totally evil. The argument requires the experience of value.

26 Aquinas, *Summa Theologiae*, I.2.3.

27 D. Hume, *Dialogues Concerning Natural Religion*, IX.

28 See Polkinghorne (1979), ch. 6.

29 Hume, op. cit., V.

30 Ps. 104.21.

31 Ps. 38.7–8.

32 See e.g. B. Davies (1982), chs. 5 and 6; Mackie (1982), chs. 5 and 8.

33 See Eigen, quoted in Peacocke (1979), p. 103.

34 Crick (1982).

35 Torrance (1985), ch. 2.

36 Torrance (1985), p. 40.

37 Reprinted in Hodgson and King (1985), p. 109.

38 Davies (1983), p. ix.

39 Polkinghorne (1986a), chs. 4 and 5.

Chapter 2 Insightful Inquiry

1 Westfall (1980), pp. 391–7.

2 See e.g. Polkinghorne (1979), ch. 7.

3 See e.g. Polkinghorne (1984).

4 Quoted in Longair (1984), p. 7.

5 Polanyi (1958).

6 A. Conan Doyle, *A Study in Scarlet*, ch. 1.

7 Pagels (1985), p. 354.

8 B. J. Carr and M. J. Rees, *Nature 278*, p. 605 (1979); see also Barrow and Tipler (1986), P. Davies (1982), Montefiore (1985).

9 See Pagels (1985), pp. 316–35.

10 P. Davies (1982), p. 130.

11 See Polkinghorne (1986b), p. 9, for a critical review.

12 Polkinghorne (1986a), ch. 5.

13 See p. 35 for discussion of a more acceptable variant of this idea.

14 Hume, op. cit., IX.

15 Kolakowski (1982), pp. 65–6.

16 For reasons for rejecting the irrational views of the nature of scientific change put forward by Kuhn and Feyerabend, see Polkinghorne (1986a), ch. 2.
17 Westfall (1980), p. 647.
18 Mackie (1982), p. 143.
19 Swinburne (1979).
20 Mackie (1982), p. 142.
21 Bartholomew (1984), p. 37. He gives in ch. 3 a critique of this approach which it will be clear I do not wholly accept.
22 Polanyi (1958), p. 33.
23 Hoyle (1983), p. 12.
24 Reprinted in Hick (1964), p. 130.
25 For a discussion of the role of induction in science see Newton-Smith (1981), *passim.*
26 Torrance (1985), p. 52.
27 See e.g. Polkinghorne (1984).
28 Lonergan (1957), p. 672.
29 Lonergan (1957), pp. 683–4.
30 Lonergan (1957), p. 636.

Chapter 3   Order and Disorder

1 See e.g. Davies (1984), Pagels (1985).
2 For a discussion of level problems see Peacocke (1979), ch. 4; Peacocke (1985); Polkinghorne (1986a), ch. 6. The last seeks to show how reductionism fails within physics itself.
3 Dawkins (1976), p. x.
4 Ward (1985), p. 64.
5 Meynell (1976), p. 85.
6 Prigogine and Stengers (1984), pp. 147–51.
7 Prigogine (1980), pp. 94–101.
8 The exception lies in a component of the weak interactions which is time-asymmetric. It has no practical consequences for present-day macroscopic processes but it played an extremely important role in the very early stages of the universe's history. Before spontaneous symmetry breaking cut the forces of nature down to their present strengths, the weak interactions were comparable in effect to the other interactions. A deep result of quantum field theory, called the TCP theorem (see Polkinghorne (1979), p. 47), links time-asymmetry with an asymmetry between matter and antimatter. This effect led to a preponderance of particles over

antiparticles in that phase of cosmic evolution, which is why the universe today is made of matter rather than antimatter.

9 Quoted in Prigogine and Stengers (1985), p. 121.

10 Quoted in Prigogine and Stengers (1985), p. 294.

11 He had to introduce the so-called cosmological term (Pais (1982), pp. 285–7), which he subsequently regretted and disowned.

12 See e.g. Feynman (1986).

13 See e.g. Polkinghorne (1984), ch. 6.

14 Prigogine and Stengers (1985), p. 16.

15 Monod (1972).

16 Prigogine and Stengers (1985), p. xxx.

17 Torrance (1985), p. 6.

18 Prigogine and Stengers (1985), ch. 9.

19 That is the origin of the celebrated fact that the gravitational three-body problem does not possess an analytic solution.

20 Prigogine and Stengers (1985), p. 271.

21 Prigogine and Stengers (1985), ch. 5.

22 Another example is the bead on the U-shaped wire, which breaks the left-right symmetry by falling to one side.

23 Bartholomew (1984), p. 95.

24 Monod (1972); Peacocke (1979), chs. 3 and 5; Polkinghorne (1986a), ch. 5.

25 Polkinghorne (1986a), p. 54.

26 Cowburn (1979).

27 Quoted in Cowburn (1979), p. 39.

28 Lonergan (1957), p. 668.

Chapter 4   Creation and Creator

1 Quoted in Hooykaas (1972), p. 41.

2 For what this implies about miracle see the discussion of Polkinghorne (1986a), pp. 74–6.

3 Hartshorne and Reese (1953).

4 Moltmann (1981), p. 106.

5 Moltmann (1981), p. 107.

6 Ps. 104.29–30.

7 C. Darwin, *The Origin of Species* (second edition), ch. 14. I am indebted to Dr Crosbie Smith for help in tracing this quotation.

8 Macquarrie (1984), p. 49.

9 Davies (1983), p. 208.

10 Davies (1983), p. 209.

11 Hoyle (1983), p. 248.

12 Teilhard de Chardin (1959).

13 Storr (1983), pp. 339–41.

14 Macquarrie (1984), p. 150.

15 Montefiore (1985), p. 161.

16 Davies (1983), p. 209.

17 Gen. 2.7.

18 Hoyle (1983), pp. 213–5; 246–8.

19 Pollard (1958).

20 Bartholomew (1984), pp. 125–33; Polkinghorne (1986a), pp. 71–2.

21 Macquarrie (1977), p. 211.

22 Polkinghorne (1979), ch. 5.

23 Augustine, *The City of God*, XI.5 and 6.

24 Pagels (1985), pp. 336–49.

25 Atkins (1981), ch. 6.

26 Cobb and Griffin (1976), p. 65.

27 Ward (1982), p. 3.

28 Ward (1982), pp. 208–9.

29 Ward (1982), p. 171. A similar understanding of God is required by consideration of prayer; see Brümmer (1984).

30 Moltmann (1981), p. 109.

31 Vanstone (1977), p. 59.

32 Vanstone (1977), pp. 62–3.

33 Bartholomew (1984), p. 145.

34 Jung (1954).

35 Pannenberg (1968), p. 165.

36 Vanstone (1977), p. 63.

37 Pannenberg (1968), p. 169.

38 Eccles. 1.2.

39 1 Cor. 15.19.

40 Rom. 8.19–21.

41 Polkinghorne (1986a), p. 81.

42 I am persuaded that Paul wrote Colossians; see Moule (1957), pp. 13–14.

43 Torrance (1976), p. 89.

44 Pannenberg (1968), p. 166.

45 Swinburne (1979), p. 103.

46 Col. 1.20.
47 Westermann (1974), p. 3.

Chapter 5   The Nature of Reality

1   Matt. 6.24.
2   Polkinghorne (1984), ch. 2.
3   Polkinghorne (1986a), p. 22. Ch. 2 presents a defence of critical realism in science; see also Newton-Smith (1981).
4   Polkinghorne (1986a), p. 92. Apparently this line of argument goes back to J. B. S. Haldane; see Popper (1982), pp. 81–2.
5   Quoted in Ward (1985), p. 34.
6   Bohr (1958), pp. 92–3.
7   Griffin (1986), p. 14.
8   Polkinghorne (1984), p. 28.
9   Griffin (1986), p. 152.
10 See Peacocke (1979), pp. 106–8; Moltmann (1985), pp. 304–7.
11 Hadamard (1945).
12 In the determinate version of quantum theory, using hidden variables, just such a divorce is made (see Bohm (1980), ch. 4; Polkinghorne (1984), pp. 56–7). In its dualism of wave and particle, Bohm's theory is a sort of quantum Cartesianism.
13 Quoted in Rucker (1982), pp. 163–4.
14 Col. 1.16.
15 Storr (1983), pp. 87–127.
16 Sheldrake (1982).
17 Polkinghorne (1984), ch. 8.
18 Popper (1979, 1982); see also Stanesby (1985), pp. 72–3.
19 Popper (1979), p. 106.
20 Popper (1979), p. 154.
21 Popper (1979), p. 112.
22 Moltmann (1985), ch. 7.
23 Moltmann (1985), p. 163.
24 Moltmann (1985), p. 166.
25 Moltmann (1985), p. 175.
26 Quoted in Leech (1985), p. 175.
27 See Rucker (1982).
28 Rucker (1982), p. 80.
29 Rucker (1982), p. 81.

30 Rucker (1982), p. 80.
31 See Trigg (1985), pp. 38–46, for a summary of gnostic beliefs.
32 Rucker (1982), pp. 161–2.
33 *The Cloud of Unknowing*, ch. 6.
34 Williams (1979), p. 169.
35 Atkins (1981) attempts the task.
36 Bohm (1980), p. 177.
37 The relation of these ideas to God's providential action will be discussed in a forthcoming book, *Providence in a Scientific Age*.

Chapter 6   Theological Science

1   Torrance (1969).
2   The position of Einstein in relation to quantum theory is curious. His interpretation of the photoelectric effect was a highly important step in the early history of the subject. However, his resolute objectivism led him later to reject the developments which led to the probability interpretation, with its consequently more elusive view of the nature of physical reality. In spirit Einstein was the last of the great classical physicists.
3   Torrance (1969), p. 131.
4   Torrance (1985), p. 19.
5   Polkinghorne (1984), ch. 2.
6   Torrance (1969), p. ix.
7   Torrance (1969), p. 12.
8   Deut. 8.16.
9   Torrance (1969), p. 287.
10 Macquarrie (1984), p. 23.
11 Torrance (1969), p. 30.
12 Torrance (1969), p. 131.
13 Polanyi (1958).
14 Theissen (1984), pp. 3–4.
15 Pais (1982), p. 113.
16 Polkinghorne (1979), pp. 43–4.
17 Theissen (1984), p. 18.
18 Farrer (1948), p. 33.
19 Farrer (1948), p. 147.
20 Rose, Kamin and Lewontin (1984), p. 237.
21 Polanyi (1958), p. 142.
22 Swinburne (1979), ch. 13.

23 Hardy (1979).

24 Carnes (1982); Newton-Smith (1981); Polkinghorne (1986a), ch. 2.

25 For my views see Polkinghorne (1983).

26 Macquarrie (1984), p. 28.

27 2 Cor. 5.17–19.

28 e.g. Mark 10.45 par; John 3.16; Acts 4.12; Heb. 5.9; 1 Pet. 1.18–20; Rev. 1.17–18.

29 Peacocke (1979), p. 240; Theissen (1984), Pt 3, ch. 3.

30 Lampe (1977).

31 Polkinghorne (1984), ch. 7.

32 Ramsey (1957), p. 136.

33 Polkinghorne (1984), pp. 48–9.

34 Capra (1975).

35 Polkinghorne (1986a), pp. 45–7.

36 Capra (1975), p. 272.

37 Frye (1982), p. 56.

38 Farrer (1948), p. 43.

39 Barbour (1974), p. 123.

40 Barbour (1974), p. 125.

41 Childs (1979), (1984).

42 Torrance (1969), p. 326.

43 John 1.14.

44 Einstein (1973), p. 55.

45 Ps. 104.24.

BIBLIOGRAPHY

Atkins, P. W. (1981), *The Creation*, W. H. Freeman.

Barbour, I. G. (1974), *Myths, Models and Paradigms*, SCM Press.

Barrow, J. D., and Tipler, F. J. (1986), *The Anthropic Cosmological Principle*, Oxford University Press.

Barth, K. (1949), E.T.: *Dogmatics in Outline*, SCM Press.

Bartholomew, D. J. (1984), *God of Chance*, SCM Press.

Bohm, D. (1980), *Wholeness and the Implicate Order*, Routledge and Kegan Paul.

Bohr, N. (1958), *Atomic Physics and Human Knowledge*, Wiley.

Brümmer, V. (1984), *What Are We Doing When We Pray?*, SCM Press.

Capra, F. (1975), *The Tao of Physics*, Wildwood House.

Carnes, J. R. (1982), *Axiomatics and Dogmatics*, Christian Journals.

Childs, B. S. (1979), *Introduction to the Old Testament as Scripture*, SCM Press.

—— (1984), *The New Testament as Canon: An Introduction*, SCM Press.

Cobb, J. B., and Griffin, D. R. (1976), *Process Theology, An Introductory Exposition*, Westminster Press.

Cowburn, J. (1979), *Shadows and the Dark*, SCM Press.

Crick, F. (1982), *Life Itself*, Macdonald.

Davies, B. (1982), *An Introduction to the Philosophy of Religion*, Oxford University Press.

Davies, P. (1982), *The Accidental Universe*, Cambridge University Press.

—— (1983), *God and the New Physics*, Dent.

—— (1984), *Superforce*, Heinemann.

Dawkins, R. (1976), *The Selfish Gene*, Oxford University Press.

Einstein, A. (1973), E.T.: *Ideas and Opinions*, Souvenir Press.

Farrer, A. (1948), *The Glass of Vision*, Dacre Press.

Feynman, R. P. (1986), *QED*, Princeton University Press.

Frye, N. (1982), *The Great Code*, Routledge and Kegan Paul.

Griffin, D. R. (ed.) (1986), *Physics and the Ultimate Significance of Time*, State University of New York Press.

Hadamard, J. (1945), *An Essay on the Psychology of Invention in the Mathematical Field*, Princeton University Press.

Hardy, A. (1979), *The Spiritual Nature of Man*, Oxford University Press.

107

Hartshorne, C., and Reese, W. L. (1953), *Philosophers Speak of God*, University of Chicago Press.

Hick, J. (1964), *The Existence of God*, Macmillan.

Hodgson, P., and King, R. (1985), *Readings in Christian Theology*, SPCK.

Hooykaas, R. (1972), *Religion and the Rise of Modern Science*, Scottish Academic Press.

Hoyle, F. (1983), *The Intelligent Universe*, Michael Joseph.

Jung, C. G. (1954), E.T.: *The Answer to Job*, Routledge and Kegan Paul.

Kolakowski, L. (1982), *Religion*, Oxford University Press.

Lampe, G. (1977), *God as Spirit*, Oxford University Press.

Leech, K. (1985), *True God*, Sheldon Press.

Lonergan, B. (1957), *Insight*, Longman.

Longair, M. (1984), *Theoretical Concepts in Physics*, Cambridge University Press.

Mackie, J. L. (1982), *The Miracle of Theism*, Oxford University Press.

Macquarrie, J. (1977), *Principles of Christian Theology* (revised edition), SCM Press.

—— (1984), *In Search of Deity*, SCM Press.

Meynell, H. A. (1976), *Introduction to the Philosophy of Bernard Lonergan*, Macmillan.

Moltmann, J. (1981), E.T.: *The Trinity and the Kingdom of God*, SCM Press.

—— (1985), E.T.: *God in Creation*, SCM Press.

Monod, J. (1972), E.T.: *Chance and Necessity*, Collins.

Montefiore, H. (1985), *The Probability of God*, SCM Press.

Moule, C. F. D. (1957), *Colossians and Philemon*, Cambridge University Press.

Newton-Smith, R. H. (1981) *The Rationality of Science*, Routledge and Kegan Paul.

Pagels, H. (1985), *Perfect Symmetry*, Michael Joseph.

Pais, A. (1982), *'Subtle is the Lord . . .'*, Oxford University Press.

Pannenberg, W. (1968), E.T.: *Jesus – God and Man*, SCM Press.

Peacocke, A. R. (1979), *Creation and the World of Science*, Oxford University Press.

—— (ed.) (1985), *Reductionism in Academic Disciplines*, SRHE & NFER Nelson.

Polanyi, M. (1958), *Personal Knowledge*, Routledge and Kegan Paul.

Polkinghorne, J. C. (1979), *The Particle Play*, W. H. Freeman.

—— (1983), *The Way the World Is*, Triangle.

—— (1984), *The Quantum World*, Longman.

—— (1986a), *One World*, SPCK.

—— (1986b), *Creation and the Structure of the Physical World*, Christian Evidence Society.

Pollard, W. G. (1958), *Chance and Providence*, Faber.

Popper, K. R. (1979), *Objective Knowledge* (revised edition), Oxford University Press.

—— (1982), *The Open Universe*, Hutchinson.

Prigogine, I. (1980), *From Being to Becoming*, W. H. Freeman.

Prigogine, I., and Stengers, I. (1984), *Order out of Chaos*, Heinemann.

Ramsey, I. T. (1957), *Religious Language*, SCM Press.

Rose, S., Kamin, L. J., and Lewontin, R. C. (1984), *Not in Our Genes*, Pantheon Books.

Rucker, R. (1982), *Infinity and the Mind*, Harvester Press.

Sheldrake, R. (1982), *A New Science of Life*, Blond and Briggs.

Snaith, J. G. (1974), *Ecclesiasticus*, Cambridge University Press.

Stanesby, D. (1985), *Science, Reason and Religion*, Croom Helm.

Storr, A. (ed.) (1983), *Jung – Selected Writings*, Fontana.

Swinburne, R. (1979), *The Existence of God*, Oxford University Press.

Teilhard de Chardin, P. (1959), *The Phenomenon of Man*, Collins.

Theissen, G. (1984), E.T.: *Biblical Faith*, SCM Press.

Torrance, T. F. (1969), *Theological Science*, Oxford University Press.

—— (1976), *Space, Time and Resurrection*, Handsel Press.

—— (1985), *Reality and Scientific Theology*, Scottish Academic Press.

Trigg, J. W. (1985), *Origen*, SCM Press.

Vanstone, W. H. (1977), *Love's Endeavour, Love's Expense*, Darton, Longman and Todd.

von Rad, G. (1972), E.T.: *Wisdom in Israel*, SCM Press.

—— (1975), E.T.: *Old Testament Theology, Vol. 1*, SCM Press.

Ward, K. (1982), *Rational Theology and the Creativity of God*, Blackwell.

—— (1985), *The Battle for the Soul*, Hodder and Stoughton.

Westerman, C. (1974), E.T.: *Creation*, SPCK.

Westfall, R. S. (1980), *Never at Rest*, Cambridge University Press.

Wiles, M. F. (1966), *The Christian Fathers*, SCM Press.

Williams, R. (1979), *The Wound of Knowledge*, Darton, Longman and Todd.

INDEX